BRITISH RAIL

ELE
MULTIF ꟷ ∪NITS

SEVENTEENTH EDITION
2004

The Complete Guide to all
Electric Multiple Units which operate on
National Rail & Eurotunnel

Peter Fox & Robert Pritchard

ISBN 1 902336 35 6

CONTENTS

PROVISION OF INFORMATION

This book has been compiled with care to be as accurate as possible, but in some cases official information is not available and the publisher cannot be held responsible for any errors or omissions. We would like to thank the companies and individuals which have been co-operative in supplying information to us. The authors of this series of books will be pleased to receive notification from readers of any inaccuracies readers may find in the series, and notification of any additional information to supplement our records and thus enhance future editions is always welcome. Please send comments to:

Robert Pritchard, Platform 5 Publishing Ltd., Wyvern House, Sark Road, Sheffield, S2 4HG, England.
Tel: 0114 255 2625 **Fax:** 0114 255 2471
e-mail: robert@platform5.com

Both the author and the staff of Platform 5 regret they are unable to answer specific queries regarding locomotives and rolling stock.

This book is updated to 17 November 2003.

UPDATES

An update to all the books in the *British Railways Pocket Book* series is published every month in the Platform 5 magazine, **entrain**, which contains news and rolling stock information on the railways of Britain and Ireland. For further details of **entrain**, please see the advertisement on the rear cover of this book.

BRITAIN'S RAILWAY SYSTEM

INFRASTRUCTURE & OPERATION

Britain's national railway infrastructure is now owned by a "not for dividend" company, Network Rail, following the demise of Railtrack. Many stations and maintenance depots are leased to and operated by Train Operating Companies (TOCs), but some larger stations remain under Network Rail control. The only exception is the infrastructure on the Isle of Wight, which is nationally owned and is leased to the Island Line franchisee.

Trains are operated by TOCs over Network Rail, regulated by access agreements between the parties involved. In general, TOCs are responsible for the provision and maintenance of the locomotives, rolling stock and staff necessary for the direct operation of services, whilst Network Rail is responsible for the provision and maintenance of the infrastructure and also for staff needed to regulate the operation of services.

DOMESTIC PASSENGER TRAIN OPERATORS

The large majority of passenger trains are operated by the TOCs on fixed term franchises. Franchise expiry dates are shown in parentheses in the list of franchisees below:

Franchise	Franchisee	Trading Name
Anglia Railways[2]	GB Railways plc. (until 4 April 2004)	Anglia Railways
Central Trains	National Express Group plc (until 1 April 2006)	Central Trains
Chiltern Railways	M40 Trains Ltd. (until December 2021)	Chiltern Railways
Cross-Country[1]	Virgin Rail Group Ltd. (until March 2012)	Virgin Trains
Gatwick Express	National Express Group plc (until 27 April 2011)	Gatwick Express
Great Eastern Railway[2]	First Group plc (until 4 April 2004)	First Great Eastern
Great Western Trains	First Group plc (until 3 February 2006)	First Great Western
InterCity East Coast	GNER Holdings Ltd. (until 4 April 2005)	Great North Eastern Railway
InterCity West Coast[1]	Virgin Rail Group Ltd. (until 8 March 2012)	Virgin Trains
Island Line	Stagecoach Holdings plc (until February 2007)	Island Line
LTS Rail	National Express Group plc (until 25 May 2011)	c2c
Merseyrail Electrics[3]	Serco/NedRail (until 20 July 2028)	Merseyrail Electrics

Midland Main Line	National Express Group plc (until 27 April 2008)	Midland Mainline
North London Railways	National Express Group plc (until 1 September 2006)	Silverlink Train Services
North West Regional Railways[4]	First Group plc (until 1 April 2004)	First North Western
Regional Railways North East[4]	Arriva Trains Ltd	Arriva Trains Northern
ScotRail	National Express Group plc (until 30 September 2004)	ScotRail
South Central	GoVia Ltd. (Go-Ahead/Keolis). (until May 2010)	South Central
South Eastern[5]		South Eastern Trains
South West	Stagecoach Holdings plc (until 3 February 2007)	South West Trains
Thames[6]	Go-Ahead Group (until 31 March 2004)	Thames Trains
Thameslink	GoVia Ltd. (until 1 April 2006)	Thameslink Rail
Wales & Borders[7]	National Express Group plc (until 6 December 2003)	Wales & Borders Trains
Wessex Trains	National Express Group plc (until 30 April 2006)	Wessex Trains
West Anglia Great Northern[8]	National Express Group plc (until 4 April 2004)	WAGN

Notes:

[1] Franchise to be renegotiated by April 2004.

[2] Due to transfer to new Greater Anglia franchise, expected to be formed in April 2004.

[3] Now under control of Merseyrail PTE instead of the Strategic Rail Authority (SRA). Franchise due to be reviewed after seven years and then every five years to fit in with Merseyside Local Transport Plan.

[4] Urban and rural services currently run by Arriva Trains Northern and First North Western are due to transfer to the new Northern franchise in late 2004. Trans-Pennine services run by these operators will be taken over by the new Trans-Pennine Express franchise on 1 February 2004.

[5] New interim management company known as South Eastern Trains (SET) formed on 9 November 2003, pending award of new Integrated Kent franchise expected in early 2005. SET is a subsidiary of the SRA.

[6] Due to transfer to First Group on 1 April 2004 for two years.

[7] Arriva Trains Ltd due to take over from National Express Group on 7 December 2003 for 15 years.

[8] West Anglia half of WAGN due to transfer to new Greater Anglia franchise. A number of options are being considered for Great Northern services, including transfer to another franchise.

GENERAL 5

A major reorganisation of franchises is under way. See **entrain** for developments.

The following operators run non-franchised services only:

Operator	Trading Name	Route
British Airports Authority	Heathrow Express	London Paddington–Heathrow Airport
Hull Trains	Hull Trains	London King's Cross–Hull
West Coast Railway Co.	West Coast Railway	Fort William–Mallaig*
		York–Scarborough*

* Special summer-dated services only.

INTERNATIONAL PASSENGER OPERATIONS

Eurostar (UK) operates international passenger-only services between the United Kingdom and continental Europe, jointly with French National Railways (SNCF) and Belgian National Railways (SNCB/NMBS). Eurostar (UK) is a subsidiary of London & Continental Railways, which is jointly owned by National Express Group plc and British Airways.

In addition, a service for the conveyance of accompanied road vehicles through the Channel Tunnel is provided by the tunnel operating company, Eurotunnel.

FREIGHT TRAIN OPERATIONS

The following operators operate freight train services under 'Open Access' arrangements:

English Welsh & Scottish Railway Ltd (EWS).
Freightliner Ltd.
GB Railfreight Ltd. (now owned by First Group)
Direct Rail Services Ltd.

INTRODUCTION

EMU CLASSES

Principal details and dimensions are quoted for each class in metric and/or imperial units as considered appropriate bearing in mind common UK usage.

All dimensions and weights are quoted for vehicles in an "as new" condition with all necessary supplies on board. Dimensions are quoted in the order length x overall width. All lengths quoted are over buffers or couplers as appropriate. Where two lengths are quoted, the first refers to outer vehicles in a set and the second to inner vehicles.

Bogie Types are quoted in the format motored/non-motored (e.g BP20/BT13 denotes BP20 motored bogies and BT non-motored bogies).

Unless noted to the contrary, all vehicles listed have bar couplings at non-driving ends.

Vehicles ordered under the auspices of BR were allocated a Lot (batch) number when ordered and these are quoted in class headings and sub-headings. Vehicles ordered since 1995 have no Lot Numbers, but the manufacturer and location that they were built is given.

NUMERICAL LISTINGS

25 kV AC 50 Hz overhead Electric Multiple Units (EMUs) and dual voltage EMUs are listed in numerical order of of set numbers. Individual 'loose' vehicles are listed in numerical order after vehicles formed into fixed formations. Where numbers carried are different to those officially allocated, these are noted in class headings where appropriate.

750 V DC third rail EMUs are listed in numerical order of class number, then in numerical order of set number. Some of these use the former Southern Region four-digit set numbers. These are derived from theoretical six digit set numbers which are the four-digit set number prefixed by the first two numbers of the class.

Where sets or vehicles have been renumbered in recent years, former numbering detail is shown alongside current detail. Each entry is laid out as in the following example:

Set No.	Detail	Livery	Owner	Operation	Allocation	Formation			
465 014	*	**CB**	H	*SE*	SG	64772	72054	72055	64822

Detail Differences. Only detail differences which currently affect the areas and types of train which vehicles may work are shown. All other detail differences are specifically excluded. Where such differences occur within a class or part class, these are shown alongside the individual set or vehicle number. Meaning of abbreviations are detailed in individual class headings.

Set Formations. Set formations shown are those normally maintained. Readers should note some set formations might be temporarily varied from time to time to suit maintenance and/or operational requirements. Vehicles shown as "Spare" are not formed in any regular set formation.

Codes. Codes are used to denote the livery, owner, operation and depot of each unit. Details of these will be found in section 6 of this book. Where a unit or spare car is off-lease, the operation column will be left blank.

Names. Only names carried with official sanction are listed. As far as possible names are shown in UPPER/lower case characters as actually shown on the name carried on the vehicle(s). Unless otherwise shown, complete units are regarded as named rather than just the individual car(s) which carry the name.

GENERAL INFORMATION

CLASSIFICATION AND NUMBERING

25 kV AC 50 Hz overhead and 'Versatile' EMUs are classified in the series 300–399.

750 V DC third rail EMUs are classified in the series 400–599.
Service units are classified in the series 900–949.

EMU individual cars are numbered in the series 61000–78999, except for vehicles used on the Isle of Wight – which are numbered in a separate series.

Prior to privatisation, Service Stock individual cars were numbered in the series 975000–975999 and 977000–977999, although this series was not used exclusively for EMU vehicles. Since privatisation, use of these series has been sporadic, vehicles often now retaining their former numbers.

Where a vehicle carries an incorrect number which duplicates another correct number, the actual number carried is shown followed by ‖ to indicate a duplicate number. Correct number details are noted in the class heading.

Any vehicle constructed or converted to replace another vehicle following accident damage and carrying the same number as the original vehicle is denoted by the suffix [2] in this publication.

OPERATING CODES

These codes are used by train operating company staff to describe the various different types of vehicles and normally appear on data panels on the inner (i.e. non driving) ends of vehicles.

A "B" prefix indicates a battery vehicle.

A "P" prefix indicates a trailer vehicle on which is mounted the pantograph, instead of the default case where the pantograph is mounted on a motor vehicle.

The first part of the code describes whether or not the car has a motor or a driving cab as follows:

DM Driving motor.
M   Motor
DT Driving trailer
T   Trailer

The next letter is a "B" for cars with a brake compartment.
This is followed by the saloon details:

F   First
S   Standard
C   Composite

The next letter denotes the style of accommodation as follows:

O   Open
K   Side compartment with lavatory
so Semi-open (part compartments, part open). All other vehicles are assumed
    to consist solely of open saloons.

Finally vehicles with a buffet are suffixed RB or RMB for a miniture buffet.

Where two vehicles of the same type are formed within the same unit, the above codes may be suffixed by (A) and (B) to differentiate between the vehicles.

A composite is a vehicle containing both first and standard class accommodation, whilst a brake vehicle is a vehicle containing separate specific accommodation for the conductor.

Special Note: Where vehicles have been declassified, the correct operating code which describes the actual vehicle layout is quoted in this publication.

The following codes are used to denote special types of vehicle:

DMLF   Driving Motor Lounge First
DMLV   Driving Motor Luggage Van
MBRBS Motor buffet standard with luggage space and guard's compartment.
TFH   Trailer First with Handbrake
TRBS   Trailer Buffet Standard

ACCOMMODATION

The information given in class headings and sub-headings is in the form F/S nT (or TD) nW. For example 12/54 1T 1W denotes 12 first class and 54 standard class seats, 1 toilet and 1 wheelchair space. The seating layout of open saloons is shown as 2+1, 2+2 or 3+2 as the case may be. Where units have first class accommodation as well as standard and the layout is different for each class then these are shown separately prefixed by '1:' and '2:'. Compartments are always three seats a side in first class and mostly four a side in standard class in EMUs.

ABBREVIATIONS

The following abbreviations are used in class headings and also throughout
this publication:

AC	Alternating Current.
BR	British Railways.
BSI	Bergische Stahl Industrie.
DC	Direct Current.
DEMU	Diesel-electric multiple unit.
DMU	Diesel multiple unit (general term).
EMU	Electric multiple unit.
Hz	Hertz.
kN	kilonewtons.
km/h	kilometres per hour.
kW	kilowatts.
LT	London Transport.
LUL	London Underground Limited.
m.	metres.
m.p.h.	miles per hour.
SR	BR Southern Region.
t.	tonnes.
V	volts.

1. 25 kV AC 50 Hz OVERHEAD & DUAL VOLTAGE UNITS.

Note: Except where otherwise stated, all units in this section operate on 25 kV AC 50 Hz overhead only.

CLASS 306   METRO-CAMMELL/BRCW

Museum unit which is not used in normal service. Originally built as 1500 V DC, but converted to AC in 1960/61.
Formation: DMSO–TBSO–DTSO.
Construction: Steel.   **Doors:** Power-operated sliding.
Traction Motors: Four Crompton-Parkinson 155 kW.
Gangways: None.   **Bogies:** LNER ED6/ET6.
Couplers: Screw.   **Maximum Speed:** 70 m.p.h.
Seating Layout: 2+2 facing.   **Dimensions:** 19.24/17.40 x 2.89 m.
Braking: Tread brakes.   **Multiple Working:** Within class.

DMSO. Lot No. 363 Metro-Cammell 1949. –/62. 51.7 t.
TBSO. Lot No. 365 BRCW 1949. –/46. 25.4 t.
DTSO. Lot No. 364 Metro-Cammell 1949. –/60. 27.9 t.

| 306 017 | **G** | H | *SS* | IL | 65217 | 65417 | 65617 |

CLASS 312   BREL YORK

Formation: BDTSO–MBSO–TSO–DTCO (* declassified).
Construction: Steel.   **Doors:** Slam.
Traction Motors: Four English Electric 546 of 201.5 kW.
Gangways: Within unit.   **Bogies:** B4.
Couplers: Buckeye.   **Maximum Speed:** 90 m.p.h.
Seating Layout: 1: 2+2 facing, 2: 3+2 facing.
Dimensions: 20.18 x 2.82 m.   **Braking:** Disc brakes.
Multiple Working: Within class.

Class 312/0. Built to operate on 25 kV 50 Hz overhead only. Of the eight units still on lease to First Great Eastern four are to be retained for use on one diagram.

76949–76974 BDTSO. Lot No. 30863 1977–1978. –/84 1T. 34.9 t.
76994–76997 BDTSO. Lot No. 30891 1976. –/84 1T. 34.9 t.
62484–62509 MBSO. Lot No. 30864 1977–1978. –/68. 56 t.
62657–62660 MBSO. Lot No. 30892 1976. –/68. 56 t.
71168–71193 TSO. Lot No. 30865 1977–1978. –/98. 30.5 t.
71277–71280 TSO. Lot No. 30893 1976. –/98. 30.5 t.
78000–78025 DTCO. Lot No. 30866 1977–1978. 25/47 1T. 33.0 t.
78045–78048 DTCO. Lot No. 30894 1976. 25/47 1T. 33.0 t.

312 701	**GE**	A	*GE*	IL	76949	62484	71168	78000
312 702	**GE**	A		PY	76950	62485	71169	78001
312 703	**GE**	A	*GE*	IL	76951	62486	71170	78002

312 704	**GE**	A		CT	76952	62487	71171	78003
312 705	**GE**	A		PY	76953	62488	71172	78004
312 706	**GE**	A		PY	76954	62489	71173	78005
312 707	**GE**	A		IL	76955	62490	71174	78006
312 708	**GE**	A		CT	76956	62491	71175	78007
312 709	**GE**	A		PY	76957	62492	71176	78008
312 710	**GE**	A		CT	76958	62493	71177	78009
312 711	**GE**	A		PY	76959	62494	71178	78010
312 712	**GE**	A		CC	76960	62495	71179	78011
312 713	**GE**	A		PY	76961	62496	71180	78012
312 714	**GE**	A	*GE*	IL	76962	62497	71181	78013
312 715	**GE**	A	*GE*	IL	76963	62498	71182	78014
312 716	**GE**	A		CT	76964	62499	71183	78015
312 717	**GE**	A		CT	76965	62500	71184	78016
312 718	**GE**	A	*GE*	IL	76966	62501	71185	78017
312 719	**GE**	A		IL	76967	62502	71186	78018
312 720	**GE**	A		CT	76968	62503	71187	78019
312 721	**GE**	A	*GE*	IL	76969	62504	71188	78020
312 722	**GE**	A	*GE*	IL	76970	62505	71189	78021
312 723	**GE**	A	*GE*	IL	76971	62506	71190	78022
312 724	**GE**	A		PY	76972	62507	71191	78023
312 725	* **N**	A		PY	76973	62509	71192	78025
312 726	* **N**	A		PY	76974	62508	71193	78024
312 727	* **N**	A		PY	76994	62657	71277	78045
312 728	* **N**	A		PY	76995	62658	71278	78046
312 729	* **N**	A		PY	76996	62659	71279	78047
312 730	* **N**	A		PY	76997	62660	71280	78048

Class 312/1. Built to operate on 25 kV or 6.25 kV 50 Hz overhead.

BDTSO. Lot No. 30867 1975–1976. –/84 2T. 34.9 t.
MBSO. Lot No. 30868 1975–1976. –/68. 56 t.
TSO. Lot No. 30869 1975–1976. –/98. 30.5 t.
DTCO. Lot No. 30870 1975–1976. 25/47 2T. 33.0 t.

312 781	* **N**	A	PY	76975	62510	71194	78026
312 782	* **N**	A	PY	76976	62511	71195	78027
312 783	* **N**	A	PY	76977	62512	71196	78028
312 784	* **N**	A	PY	76978	62513	71197	78029
312 785	* **N**	A	PY	76979	62514	71198	78030
312 786	* **N**	A	PY	76980	62515	71199	78031
312 787	* **N**	A	PY	76981	62516	71200	78032
312 788	* **N**	A	PY	76982	62517	71201	78033
312 789	* **N**	A	PY	76983	62518	71202	78034
312 790	* **N**	A	PY	76984	62519	71203	78035
312 791	* **N**	A	PY	76985	62520	71204	78036
312 792	* **N**	A	PY	76986	62521	71205	78037
312 793	* **N**	A	PY	76987	62522	71206	78038
312 794	* **N**	A	PY	76988	62523	71207	78039
312 795	* **N**	A	PY	76989	62524	71208	78040
312 796	* **N**	A	PY	76990	62525	71209	78041
312 797	* **N**	A	PY	76991	62526	71210	78042

312 798	* **N**	A	PY	76992	62527	71211	78043
312 799	* **N**	A	PY	76993	62528	71212	78044

CLASS 313   BREL YORK

WAGN/Silverlink inner suburban units.
Formation: DMSO–PTSO–BDMSO.
Systems: 25 kV AC overhead/750 V DC third rail.
Construction: Steel underframe, aluminium alloy body and roof.
Traction Motors: Four GEC G310AZ of 82.125 kW.
Doors: Sliding.   **Control System:** Camshaft.
Gangways: Within unit + end doors.   **Bogies:** BX1.
Couplers: Tightlock   **Maximum Speed:** 75 m.p.h.
Seating Layout: 3+2 facing.   **Dimensions:** 20.18 x 2.82 m.
Braking: Disc and rheostatic.   **Multiple Working:** Within class.

DMSO. Lot No. 30879 1976–1977. –/74. 36.4 t.
PTSO. Lot No. 30880 1976–1977. –/84 (313/0), –/80 (313/1). 30.5 t.
BDMSO. Lot No. 30885 1976–1977. –/74. 37.6 t.

Advertising Liveries: 313 027, 313 043, 313 050, 313 057, 313 064 WAGN Family
Travelcard ("Go to town with WAGN") – White.
313 060, WAGN "Intalink" livery – White with a yellow and green bodyside stripe.

Class 313/0. Standard Design. All now refurbished with high back seats.

313 018	**WP**	H	*WN*	HE	62546	71230	62610
313 024	**WP**	H	*WN*	HE	62552	71236	62616
313 025	**N**	H	*WN*	HE	62553	71237	62617
313 026	**N**	H	*WN*	HE	62554	71238	62618
313 027	**AL**	H	*WN*	HE	62555	71239	62619
313 028	**WP**	H	*WN*	HE	62556	71240	62620
313 029	**U**	H	*WN*	HE	62557	71241	62621
313 030	**WP**	H	*WN*	HE	62558	71242	62622
313 031	**WP**	H	*WN*	HE	62559	71243	62623
313 032	**U**	H	*WN*	HE	62560	71244	62643
313 033	**U**	H	*WN*	HE	62561	71245	62625
313 035	**U**	H	*WN*	HE	62563	71247	62627
313 036	**U**	H	*WN*	HE	62564	71248	62628
313 037	**U**	H	*WN*	HE	62565	71249	62629
313 038	**U**	H	*WN*	HE	62566	71250	62630
313 039	**U**	H	*WN*	HE	62567	71251	62631
313 040	**U**	H	*WN*	HE	62568	71252	62632
313 041	**U**	H	*WN*	HE	62569	71253	62633
313 042	**N**	H	*WN*	HE	62570	71254	62634
313 043	**AL**	H	*WN*	HE	62571	71255	62635
313 044	**U**	H	*WN*	HE	62572	71256	62636
313 045	**U**	H	*WN*	HE	62573	71257	62637
313 046	**U**	H	*WN*	HE	62574	71258	62638
313 047	**U**	H	*WN*	HE	62575	71259	62639
313 048	**N**	H	*WN*	HE	62576	71260	62640
313 049	**U**	H	*WN*	HE	62577	71261	62641

313 050	**AL**	H	*WN*	HE	62578	71262	62649
313 051	**U**	H	*WN*	HE	62579	71263	62624
313 052	**N**	H	*WN*	HE	62580	71264	62644
313 053	**N**	H	*WN*	HE	62581	71265	62645
313 054	**N**	H	*WN*	HE	62582	71266	62646
313 055	**N**	H	*WN*	HE	62583	71267	62647
313 056	**WP**	H	*WN*	HF	62584	71268	62648
313 057	**AL**	H	*WN*	HE	62585	71269	62642
313 058	**N**	H	*WN*	HE	62586	71270	62650
313 059	**N**	H	*WN*	HE	62587	71271	62651
313 060	**AL**	H	*WN*	HE	62588	71272	62652
313 061	**N**	H	*WN*	HE	62589	71273	62653
313 062	**N**	H	*WN*	HE	62590	71274	62654
313 063	**N**	H	*WN*	HE	62591	71275	62655
313 064	**AL**	H	*WN*	HE	62592	71276	62656

Class 313/1. Extra shoegear for Silverlink services.

313 101	**SL**	H	*SL*	BY	62529	71213	62593
313 102	**SL**	H	*SL*	BY	62530	71214	62594
313 103	**SL**	H	*SL*	BY	62531	71215	62595
313 104	**SL**	H	*SL*	BY	62532	71216	62596
313 105	**SL**	H	*SL*	BY	62533	71217	62597
313 106	**SL**	H	*SL*	BY	62534	71218	62598
313 107	**SL**	H	*SL*	BY	62535	71219	62599
313 108	**SL**	H	*SL*	BY	62536	71220	62600
313 109	**SL**	H	*SL*	BY	62537	71221	62601
313 110	**SL**	H	*SL*	BY	62538	71222	62602
313 111	**SL**	H	*SL*	BY	62539	71223	62603
313 112	**SL**	H	*SL*	BY	62540	71224	62604
313 113	**SL**	H	*SL*	BY	62541	71225	62605
313 114	**SL**	H	*SL*	BY	62542	71226	62606
313 115	**SL**	H	*SL*	BY	62543	71227	62607
313 116	**SL**	H	*SL*	BY	62544	71228	62608
313 117	**SL**	H	*SL*	BY	62545	71229	62609
313 119	**SL**	H	*SL*	BY	62547	71231	62611
313 120	**SL**	H	*SL*	BY	62548	71232	62612
313 121	**SL**	H	*SL*	BY	62549	71233	62613
313 122	**SL**	H	*SL*	BY	62550	71234	62614
313 123	**SL**	H	*SL*	BY	62551	71235	62615
313 134	**SL**	H	*SL*	BY	62562	71246	62626

Names (carried on PTSO):

313 109	Arnold Leah	313 116	Nikola Tesla
313 120	PARLIAMENT HILL.		

CLASS 314   BREL YORK

ScotRail inner suburban units.
Formation: DMSO–PTSO–DMSO.
Construction: Steel underframe, aluminium alloy body and roof.
Traction Motors: Four GEC G310AZ (* Brush TM61-53) of 82.125 kW.

Doors: Sliding.
Gangways: Within unit + end doors.
Couplers: Tightlock
Seating Layout: 3+2 facing.
Braking: Disc and rheostatic.
Multiple Working: Within class and with Class 315.
Control System: Thyristor.
Bogies: BX1.
Maximum Speed: 75 m.p.h.
Dimensions: 20.18 x 2.82 m.

64583–64614. DMSO. Lot No. 30912 1979. –/68. 34.5 t.
64588ⁿ. DMSO. Lot No. 30908 1978–1980. Rebuilt Railcare Glasgow 1996 from Class 507 No. 64426. The original 64588 has been scrapped. This vehicle has an experimental seating layout. –/74. 35.63 t.
PTSO. Lot No. 30913 1979. –/76. 33.0 t.

314 201	*	S	A	SR	GW	64583	71450	64584
314 202	*	S	A	SR	GW	64585	71451	64586
314 203	*	SC	A	SR	GW	64587	71452	64588ⁿ
314 204	*	SC	A	SR	GW	64589	71453	64590
314 205	*	SC	A	SR	GW	64591	71454	64592
314 206	*	SC	A	SR	GW	64593	71455	64594
314 207		S	A	SR	GW	64595	71456	64596
314 208		SC	A	SR	GW	64597	71457	64598
314 209		S	A	SR	GW	64599	71458	64600
314 210		SC	A	SR	GW	64601	71459	64602
314 211		SC	A	SR	GW	64603	71460	64604
314 212		SC	A	SR	GW	64605	71461	64606
314 213		S	A	SR	GW	64607	71462	64608
314 214		S	A	SR	GW	64609	71463	64610
314 215		SC	A	SR	GW	64611	71464	64612
314 216		SC	A	SR	GW	64613	71465	64614

Name (carried on PTSO):

314 203   European Union

CLASS 315   BREL YORK

FGE/WAGN inner suburban units.
Formation: DMSO–TSO–PTSO–DMSO.
Construction: Steel underframe, aluminium alloy body and roof.
Traction Motors: Four Brush TM61-53 (* GEC G310AZ) of 82.125 kW.
Doors: Sliding.
Gangways: Within unit + end doors.
Couplers: Tightlock
Seating Layout: 3+2 facing.
Braking: Disc and rheostatic.
Control System: Thyristor.
Bogies: BX1.
Maximum Speed: 75 m.p.h.
Dimensions: 20.18 x 2.82 m.
Multiple Working: Within class and with Class 314.
64461–64582. DMSO. Lot No. 30902 1980–1981. –/74. 35 t.
71281–71341. TSO. Lot No. 30904 1980–1981. –/86. 25.5 t.
71389–71449. PTSO. Lot No. 30903 1980–1981. –/84. 32 t.

Advertising Liveries: 315 844, 315 845 WAGN Family Travelcard ("Go to town with WAGN") – White.
315 857 WAGN "Intalink" livery – White with a yellow and green bodyside stripe.

315 801		**GE**	H	*GE*	IL	64461	71281	71389	64462
315 802		**GE**	H	*GE*	IL	64463	71282	71390	64464
315 803		**GE**	H	*GE*	IL	64465	71283	71391	64466
315 804		**GE**	H	*GE*	IL	64467	71284	71392	64468
315 805		**GE**	H	*GE*	IL	64469	71285	71393	64470
315 806		**GE**	H	*GE*	IL	64471	71286	71394	64472
315 807		**GE**	H	*GE*	IL	64473	71287	71395	64474
315 808		**GE**	H	*GE*	IL	64475	71288	71396	64476
315 809		**GE**	H	*GE*	IL	64477	71289	71397	64478
315 810		**GE**	H	*GE*	IL	64479	71290	71398	64480
315 811		**GE**	H	*GE*	IL	64481	71291	71399	64482
315 812		**GE**	H	*GE*	IL	64483	71292	71400	64484
315 813		**GE**	H	*GE*	IL	64485	71293	71401	64486
315 814		**GE**	H	*GE*	IL	64487	71294	71402	64488
315 815		**GE**	H	*GE*	IL	64489	71295	71403	64490
315 816		**GE**	H	*GE*	IL	64491	71296	71404	64492
315 817		**GE**	H	*GE*	IL	64493	71297	71405	64494
315 818		**GE**	H	*GE*	IL	64495	71298	71406	64496
315 819		**GE**	H	*GE*	IL	64497	71299	71407	64498
315 820		**GE**	H	*GE*	IL	64499	71300	71408	64500
315 821		**GE**	H	*GE*	IL	64501	71301	71409	64502
315 822		**GE**	H	*GE*	IL	64503	71302	71410	64504
315 823		**GE**	H	*GE*	IL	64505	71303	71411	64506
315 824		**GE**	H	*GE*	IL	64507	71304	71412	64508
315 825		**GE**	H	*GE*	IL	64509	71305	71413	64510
315 826		**GE**	H	*GE*	IL	64511	71306	71414	64512
315 827		**GE**	H	*GE*	IL	64513	71307	71415	64514
315 828		**GE**	H	*GE*	IL	64515	71308	71416	64516
315 829		**GE**	H	*GE*	IL	64517	71309	71417	64518
315 830		**GE**	H	*GE*	IL	64519	71310	71418	64520
315 831		**GE**	H	*GE*	IL	64521	71311	71419	64522
315 832		**GE**	H	*GE*	IL	64523	71312	71420	64524
315 833		**GE**	H	*GE*	IL	64525	71313	71421	64526
315 834		**GE**	H	*GE*	IL	64527	71314	71422	64528
315 835		**GE**	H	*GE*	IL	64529	71315	71423	64530
315 836		**GE**	H	*GE*	IL	64531	71316	71424	64532
315 837		**GE**	H	*GE*	IL	64533	71317	71425	64534
315 838		**GE**	H	*GE*	IL	64535	71318	71426	64536
315 839		**GE**	H	*GE*	IL	64537	71319	71427	64538
315 840		**GE**	H	*GE*	IL	64539	71320	71428	64540
315 841		**GE**	H	*GE*	IL	64541	71321	71429	64542
315 842	*	**GE**	H	*GE*	IL	64543	71322	71430	64544
315 843	*	**GE**	H	*GE*	IL	64545	71323	71431	64546
315 844	*	**AL**	H	*WN*	HE	64547	71324	71432	64548
315 845	*	**AL**	H	*WN*	HE	64549	71325	71433	64550
315 846	*	**U**	H	*WN*	HE	64551	71326	71434	64552
315 847	*	**U**	H	*WN*	HE	64553	71327	71435	64554
315 848	*	**U**	H	*WN*	HE	64555	71328	71436	64556
315 849	*	**U**	H	*WN*	HE	64557	71329	71437	64558
315 850	*	**U**	H	*WN*	HE	64559	71330	71438	64560
315 851	*	**U**	H	*WN*	HE	64561	71331	71439	64562

315 852	*	U	H	WN	HE	64563	71332	71440	64564
315 853	*	U	H	WN	HE	64565	71333	71441	64566
315 854	*	U	H	WN	HE	64567	71334	71442	64568
315 855	*	U	H	WN	HE	64569	71335	71443	64570
315 856	*	U	H	WN	HE	64571	71336	71444	64572
315 857	*	AL	H	WN	HE	64573	71337	71445	64574
315 858	*	U	H	WN	HE	64579	71338	71446	64580
315 859	*	WP	H	WN	HE	64577	71339	71447	64578
315 860	*	WP	H	WN	HE	64575	71340	71448	64576
315 861	*	WP	H	WN	HE	64581	71341	71449	64582

CLASS 317   BREL

WAGN outer suburban units.
Formations: Various.
Construction: Steel.
Traction Motors: Four GEC G315BZ of 247.5 kW.
Doors: Sliding.   **Control System:** Thyristor.
Gangways: Throughout   **Bogies:** BP20 (MSO), BT13 (others).
Couplers: Tightlock.   **Maximum Speed:** 100 m.p.h.
Seating Layout: Various.   **Dimensions:** 20.13/20.18 x 2.82 m.
Braking: Disc.
Multiple Working: Within class and with Classes 318, 319, 320, 321, 322 and 323.

Class 317/1. Pressure ventilated.

Formation: DTSO(A)–MSO–TCO–DTSO(B).
Seating Layout: 1: 2+2 facing, 2: 3+2 facing.

DTSO(A) Lot No. 30955 York 1981–1982. –/74. 29.44 t.
MSO. Lot No. 30958 York 1981–1982. –/79. 49.76 t.
TCO. Lot No. 30957 Derby 1981–1982. 22/46 2T. 28.80 t. Retention toilets (decommissioned).
DTSO(B) Lot No. 30956 York 1981–1982. –/70. (* –/71). 29.28 t.

Non-standard livery: 317 301–317 306 are in the former LTS Rail livery (white & blue with grey & green bands).

317 301	0	A	WN	HE	77024	62661	71577	77048
317 302	0	A	WN	HE	77001	62662	71578	77049
317 303	0	A	WN	HE	77002	62663	71579	77050
317 304	0	A	WN	HE	77003	62664	71580	77051
317 305	0	A	WN	HE	77004	62665	71581	77052
317 306	0	A	WN	HE	77005	62666	71582	77053
317 307	WP	A	WN	HE	77006	62667	71583	77054
317 311	WP	A	WN	HE	77010	62697	71587	77058
317 312	WP	A	WN	HE	77011	62672	71588	77059
317 313	WP	A	WN	HE	77012	62673	71589	77060
317 315	WP	A	WN	HE	77014	62675	71591	77062
317 316	N	A	WN	HE	77015	62676	71592	77063
317 317	WP	A	WN	HE	77016	62677	71593	77064
317 318	WP	A	WN	HE	77017	62678	71594	77065
317 320	WP	A	WN	HE	77019	62680	71596	77067

▲ 312 721 is seen passing Pudding Mill Lane at the head of a 12-car e.c.s. working ready to form a First Great Eastern peak hour commuter service on 06/05/03. The remaining FGE 312s now only have one booked diagram – a peak hour commuter service.   **Alex Dasi-Sutton**

▼ Wearing the new West Anglia Great Northern livery, 313 024 calls at Hitchin on 16/08/02.   **Mervyn Turvey**

▲ Strathclyde PTE-liveried 314 211 is seen at Neilston prior to forming the 12.27 to Glasgow Central on 14/03/03. **Robert Pritchard**

▼ 317 331 is seen in the new WAGN purple livery at Huntingdon. **Doug Birmingham**

▲ Connex-liveried 319 216 passes Salfords on the 15.08 London Victoria–Brighton "Brighton Express" service on 31/08/01. This service is now mainly worked by Class 377s.   **Rodney Lissenden**

▼ 320 320 is seen at Milngavie waiting to form the 15.22 to Springburn on 14/03/03.   **Alan Yearsley**

Still in Stansted Skytrain livery, 322 485 is seen near Kingston, East Lothian with the 11.20 North Berwick–Edinburgh Waverley on 10/09/03. **Adrian T. Sumner**

▲ Silverlink-liveried 321 433 and 321 404 approach Milton Keynes Central with the 16.39 London Euston–Rugby on 08/06/03. **Mark Beal**

▼ Centro-liveried 323 218 passes Slindon, Staffs on 27/03/03 working the 15.32 Birmingham New Street–Liverpool Lime Street. **Bob Sweet**

▲ Royal Mail-liveried 325 004 is seen near Kensington Olympia with 5O04 11.35 Willesden Railnet–Tonbridge on 23/01/03.   **Alex Dasi-Sutton**

▼ West Yorkshire PTE-liveried 333 001 at Bradford Forster Square prior to forming the 17.02 to Leeds on 19/07/03.   **Robert Pritchard**

▲ One of the stylish-looking Class 334s No. 334 019 enters Paisley Gilmour Street with an Ayr–Glasgow Central working on 18/02/03. **Jonathan M. Allen**

▼ c2c-liveried 357 228 at Ockendon with the 15.50 London Fenchurch Street–Pitsea on 18/04/03. **Paul Shannon**

▲ Siemens Desiro 360 119 departs Mistley on 16/09/03 with the 14.46 Manningtree–Harwich Town. These units are intended for First Great Eastern's London Liverpool Street–Ipswich/Clacton services, and the Harwich branch will then be worked by 15-year-old Class 321s. **Bob Sweet**

▼ New Connex-liveried Class 375 "Electrostar" unit 375 617 passes Chartham with a Ramsgate-bound e.c.s. working on 26/07/02. **Colin Scott-Morton**

317 321	WP	A	WN	HE	77020	62681	71597	77068
317 324	N	A	WN	HE	77023	62684	71600	77071
317 325	WP	A	WN	HE	77000	62685	71601	77072
317 326	N	A	WN	HE	77025	62686	71602	77073
317 327	N	A	WN	HE	77026	62687	71603	77074
317 328	N	A	WN	HE	77027	62688	71604	77075
317 330	WP	A	WN	HE	77043	62704	71606	77077
317 331	WP	A	WN	HE	77030	62691	71607	77078
317 333	WP	A	WN	HE	77032	62693	71609	77080
317 334	WP	A	WN	HE	77033	62694	71610	77081
317 335	WP	A	WN	HE	77034	62695	71611	77082
317 336	WP	A	WN	HE	77035	62696	71612	77083
317 337 *	WP	A	WN	HE	77036	62671	71613	77084
317 338 *	WP	A	WN	HE	77037	62698	71614	77085
317 339 *	WP	A	WN	HE	77038	62699	71615	77086
317 340 *	WP	A	WN	HE	77039	62700	71616	77087
317 341 *	WP	A	WN	HE	77040	62701	71617	77088
317 342 *	WP	A	WN	HE	77041	62702	71618	77089
317 343 *	WP	A	WN	HE	77042	62703	71619	77090
317 344 *	N	A	WN	HE	77029	62690	71620	77091
317 345 *	N	A	WN	HE	77044	62705	71621	77092
317 346 *	N	A	WN	HE	77045	62706	71622	77093
317 347 *	N	A	WN	HE	77046	62707	71623	77094
317 348 *	WP	A	WN	HE	77047	62708	71624	77095

Name (carried on TCO):

317 348   Richard A Jenner

Class 317/6. Convection heating. Units converted from Class 317/2 by Railcare Wolverton 1998–99 with new seating layouts.

Formation: DTSO–MSO–TSO–DTCO.
Seating Layout: 2+2 facing.

77200–77219. DTSO. Lot No. 30994 York 1985–1986. –/64. 29.31 t.
77280–77283. DTSO. Lot No. 31007 York 1987. –/64. 29.31 t.
62846–62865. MSO. Lot No. 30996 York 1985–1986. –/70. 50.08 t.
62886–62889. MSO. Lot No. 31009 York 1987. –/70. 50.08 t.
71734–71753. TSO. Lot No. 30997 York 1985–1986. –/62 2T. 28.28 t.
71762–71765. TSO. Lot No. 31010 York 1987. –/62 2T. 28.28 t.
77220–77239. DTCO. Lot No. 30995 York 1985–1986. 24/48. 29.28 t.
77284–77287. DTCO. Lot No. 31008 York 1987. 24/48. 29.28 t.

317 649	WN	A	WN	HE	77200	62846	71734	77220
317 650	WN	A	WN	HE	77201	62847	71735	77221
317 651	WN	A	WN	HE	77202	62848	71736	77222
317 652	WN	A	WN	HE	77203	62849	71739	77223
317 653	WN	A	WN	HE	77204	62850	71738	77224
317 654	WN	A	WN	HE	77205	62851	71737	77225
317 655	WN	A	WN	HE	77206	62852	71740	77226
317 656	WN	A	WN	HE	77207	62853	71742	77227
317 657	WN	A	WN	HE	77208	62854	71741	77228
317 658	WN	A	WN	HE	77209	62855	71743	77229

317 659	**WN**	A	*WN*	HE	77210	62856	71744	77230
317 660	**WN**	A	*WN*	HE	77211	62857	71745	77231
317 661	**WN**	A	*WN*	HE	77212	62858	71746	77232
317 662	**WN**	A	*WN*	HE	77213	62859	71747	77233
317 663	**WN**	A	*WN*	HE	77214	62860	71748	77234
317 664	**WN**	A	*WN*	HE	77215	62861	71749	77235
317 665	**WN**	A	*WN*	HE	77216	62862	71750	77236
317 666	**WN**	A	*WN*	HE	77217	62863	71752	77237
317 667	**WN**	A	*WN*	HE	77218	62864	71751	77238
317 668	**WN**	A	*WN*	HE	77219	62865	71753	77239
317 669	**WN**	A	*WN*	HE	77280	62886	71762	77284
317 670	**WN**	A	*WN*	HE	77281	62887	71763	77285
317 671	**WN**	A	*WN*	HE	77282	62888	71764	77286
317 672	**WN**	A	*WN*	HE	77283	62889	71765	77207

Class 317/7. Units converted from Class 317/1 by Railcare Wolverton 2000 for Stansted Express service between London Liverpool Street and Stansted. Air conditioning. Fitted with luggage stacks.

Formation: DTSO–MSO–TSO–DTCO.
Seating Layout: 1: 2+1 facing 2: 2+2 facing.

DTSO Lot No. 30955 York 1981–1982. –/52 + catering point. 29.44 t.
MSO. Lot No. 30958 York 1981–1982. –/62. 49.76 t.
TSO. Lot No. 30957 Derby 1981–1982. –/42 1W 1T 1TD. 28.80 t. Retention toilets (decommissioned).
DTCO Lot No. 30956 York 1981–1982. 22/16 + catering point. 29.28 t.

317 708	**SX**	A	*WN*	HE	77007	62668	71584	77055
317 709	**SX**	A	*WN*	HE	77008	62669	71585	77056
317 710	**SX**	A	*WN*	HE	77009	62670	71586	77057
317 714	**SX**	A	*WN*	HE	77013	62674	71590	77061
317 719	**SX**	A	*WN*	HE	77018	62679	71595	77066
317 722	**SX**	A	*WN*	HE	77021	62682	71598	77069
317 723	**SX**	A	*WN*	HE	77022	62683	71599	77070
317 729	**SX**	A	*WN*	HE	77028	62689	71605	77076
317 732	**SX**	A	*WN*	HE	77031	62692	71608	77079

Name (carried on DTCO):

317 723   The Tottenham Flyer

CLASS 318   BREL YORK

ScotRail outer suburban units.
Formation: DTSO–MSO–DTSO.
Construction: Steel.
Traction Motors: Four Brush TM 2141 of 268 kW.
Doors: Sliding.
Gangways: Throughout.
Couplers: Tightlock.
Seating Layout: 3+2 facing.
Control System: Thyristor.
Bogies: BP20 (MSO), BT13 (others).
Maximum Speed: 90 m.p.h.
Dimensions: 20.18 x 2.82 m.

Braking: Disc.
Multiple Working: Within class and with Classes 317, 319, 320, 321, 322 and 323.

77240–77259. DTSO. Lot No. 30999 1985–1986. –/66 1T. 30.01 t.
77288. DTSO. Lot No. 31020 1987. –/66 1T. 30.01 t.
62866–62885. MSO. Lot No. 30998 1985–1986. –/79. 50.90 t.
62890. MSO. Lot No. 31019 1987. –/79. 50.90 t.
77260–77279. DTSO. Lot No. 31000 1985–1986. –/71. 26.60 t.
77289. DTSO. Lot No. 31021 1987. –/71. 26.60 t.

318 250	**SC**	H	*SR*	GW	77240	62866	77260
318 251	**SC**	H	*SR*	GW	77241	62867	77261
318 252	**SC**	H	*SR*	GW	77242	62868	77262
318 253	**SC**	H	*SR*	GW	77243	62869	77263
318 254	**SC**	H	*SR*	GW	77244	62870	77264
318 255	**SC**	H	*SR*	GW	77245	62871	77265
318 256	**SC**	H	*SR*	GW	77246	62872	77266
318 257	**SC**	H	*SR*	GW	77247	62873	77267
318 258	**SC**	H	*SR*	GW	77248	62874	77268
318 259	**SC**	H	*SR*	GW	77249	62875	77269
318 260	**SC**	H	*SR*	GW	77250	62876	77270
318 261	**SC**	H	*SR*	GW	77251	62877	77271
318 262	**SC**	H	*SR*	GW	77252	62878	77272
318 263	**SC**	H	*SR*	GW	77253	62879	77273
318 264	**SC**	H	*SR*	GW	77254	62880	77274
318 265	**SC**	H	*SR*	GW	77255	62881	77275
318 266	**SC**	H	*SR*	GW	77256	62882	77276
318 267	**SC**	H	*SR*	GW	77257	62883	77277
318 268	**SC**	H	*SR*	GW	77258	62884	77278
318 269	**SC**	H	*SR*	GW	77259	62885	77279
318 270	**SC**	H	*SR*	GW	77288	62890	77289

Names (carried on MSO):

318 259	Citizens' Network	318 266 STRATHCLYDER.

CLASS 319   BREL YORK

System: 25 kV AC overhead/750 V DC third rail.
Formation: Various.
Construction: Steel.
Traction Motors: Four GEC G315BZ of 268 kW.
Doors: Sliding.   **Control System:** GTO chopper.
Gangways: Within unit + end doors.   **Bogies:** P7-4 (MSO), T3-7 (others).
Couplers: Tightlock   **Maximum Speed:** 100 m.p.h.
Seating Layout: Various.   **Dimensions:** 20.18 x 2.82 m.
Braking: Disc.
Multiple Working: Within class and with Classes 317, 318, 320, 321, 322 and 323.

Class 319/0. DTSO(A)–MSO–TSO–DTSO(B). South Central/Thameslink units.
Seating Layout: 3+2 facing.

DTSO(A). Lot No. 31022 (odd nos.) 1987–1988. –/82. 30.12 t.
MSO. Lot No. 31023 1987–1988. –/82. 51 t.
TSO. Lot No. 31024 1987–1988. –/77 2T. 51 t.
DTSO(B). Lot No. 31025 (even nos.) 1987–1988. –/78. 30 t.

319 001	**CX**	P	*TR*	SU	77291	62891	71772	77290
319 002	**CX**	P	*TR*	SU	77293	62892	71773	77292
319 003	**CX**	P	*TR*	SU	77295	62893	71774	77294
319 004	**CX**	P	*TR*	SU	77297	62894	71775	77296
319 005	**CX**	P	*TR*	SU	77299	62895	71776	77298
319 006	**CX**	P	*SC*	SU	77301	62896	71777	77300
319 007	**CX**	P	*SC*	SU	77303	62897	71778	77302
319 008	**CX**	P	*SC*	SU	77305	62898	71779	77304
319 009	**CX**	P	*SC*	SU	77307	62899	71780	77306
319 010	**CX**	P	*SC*	SU	77309	62900	71781	77308
319 011	**CX**	P	*SC*	SU	77311	62901	71782	77310
319 012	**CX**	P	*SC*	SU	77313	62902	71783	77312
319 013	**CX**	P	*SC*	SU	77315	62903	71784	77314

Names (carried on TSO):

319 008	Cheriton		319 011	John Ruskin College
319 009	Coquelles		319 013	The Surrey Hills

Class 319/2. DTSO–MSO–TSO–DTCO. Units converted from Class 319/0 for South Central express services from London to Brighton. Pantographs refitted for use with Thameslink or on South Central's Watford–Gatwick Airport services.

Seating Layout: 1: 2+1 facing, 2: 2+2 facing.

DTSO. Lot No. 31022 (odd nos.) 1987–1988. –/64. 30.2 t.
MSO. Lot No. 31023 1987–1988. –/60 2T. (including 12 seats in a "snug" under the pantograph area). External sliding doors sealed adjacent to this area. 51.0 t.
TSO. Lot No. 31024 1987–1988. –/52 1T 1TD. 34 t.
DTCO. Lot No. 31025 (even nos.) 1987–1988. 18/36. 30 t.

Advertising Livery: 319 214, 319 215, 319 218, 319 220 Connex Days out/"Family Zone" (Yellow, green and red with various images).

319 214	**AL**	P	*TR*	SU	77317	62904	71785	77316
319 215	**AL**	P	*SC*	SU	77319	62905	71786	77318
319 216	**CX**	P	*SC*	SU	77321	62906	71787	77320
319 217	**CX**	P	*SC*	SU	77323	62907	71788	77322
319 218	**AL**	P	*SC*	SU	77325	62908	71789	77324
319 219	**CX**	P	*SC*	SU	77327	62909	71790	77326
319 220	**AL**	P	*SC*	SU	77329	62910	71791	77328

Names (carried on TSO):

319 215	London		319 218	Croydon.
319 217	Brighton			

Class 319/3. DTSO(A)–MSO–TSO–DTSO(B). Thameslink units. Converted from Class 319/1 by replacing first class seats with standard class seats. Used mainly on the Luton–Sutton route.

Seating Layout: 3+2 facing.

DTSO(A). Lot No. 31063 1990. –/70. 29.0 t.
MSO. Lot No. 31064 1990. –/78. 50.6 t.
TSO. Lot No. 31065 1990. –/74 2T. 31.0 t.
DTSO(B). Lot No. 31066 1990. –/78. 29.7 t.

319 361	**TR**	P	*TR*	SU	77459	63043	71929	77458
319 362	**TR**	P	*TR*	SU	77461	63044	71930	77460
319 363	**TR**	P	*TR*	SU	77463	63045	71931	77462
319 364	**TR**	P	*TR*	SU	77465	63046	71932	77464
319 365	**TR**	P	*TR*	SU	77467	63047	71933	77466
319 366	**TR**	P	*TR*	SU	77469	63048	71934	77468
319 367	**TR**	P	*TR*	SU	77471	63049	71935	77470
319 368	**TR**	P	*TR*	SU	77473	63050	71936	77472
319 369	**TR**	P	*TR*	SU	77475	63051	71937	77474
319 370	**TR**	P	*TR*	SU	77477	63052	71938	77476
319 371	**TR**	P	*TR*	SU	77479	63053	71939	77478
319 372	**TR**	P	*TR*	SU	77481	63054	71940	77480
319 373	**TR**	P	*TR*	SU	77483	63055	71941	77482
319 374	**TR**	P	*TR*	SU	77485	63056	71942	77484
319 375	**TR**	P	*TR*	SU	77487	63057	71943	77486
319 376	**TR**	P	*TR*	SU	77489	63058	71944	77488
319 377	**TR**	P	*TR*	SU	77491	63059	71945	77490
319 378	**TR**	P	*TR*	SU	77493	63060	71946	77492
319 379	**TR**	P	*TR*	SU	77495	63061	71947	77494
319 380	**TR**	P	*TR*	SU	77497	63062	71948	77496
319 381	**TR**	P	*TR*	SU	77973	63093	71979	77974
319 382	**TR**	P	*TR*	SU	77975	63094	71980	77976
319 383	**TR**	P	*TR*	SU	77977	63095	71981	77978
319 384	**TR**	P	*TR*	SU	77979	63096	71982	77980
319 385	**TR**	P	*TR*	SU	77981	63097	71983	77982
319 386	**TR**	P	*TR*	SU	77983	63098	71984	77984

Class 319/4. DTCO–MSO–TSO–DTSO. Thameslink units. Converted from Class 319/0. Refurbished with carpets. DTSO(A) converted to composite. Used mainly on the Bedford–Gatwick–Brighton route.

Seating Layout: 1: 2+2 facing 2: 3+2 facing.

77331–77381. DTCO. Lot No. 31022 (odd nos.) 1987–1988. 12/54. 30.1 t.
77431–77457. DTCO. Lot No. 31038 (odd nos.) 1988. 12/54. 30.1 t.
62911–92936. MSO. Lot No. 31023 1987–1988. –/77. 51.0 t.
62961–92974. MSO. Lot No. 31039 1988. –/77. 51.0 t.
71792–71817. TSO. Lot No. 31024 1987–1988. –/72 2T. 51.0 t.
71866–71879. TSO. Lot No. 31040 1988. –/72 2T. 51.0 t.
77330–77380. DTSO. Lot No. 31025 (even nos.) 1987–1988. –/74. 30.0 t.
77430–77456. DTSO. Lot No. 31041 (even nos.) 1988. –/74. 30.0 t.

319 421	**TR**	P	*TR*	SU	77331	62911	71792	77330
319 422	**TR**	P	*TR*	SU	77333	62912	71793	77332
319 423	**TR**	P	*TR*	SU	77335	62913	71794	77334
319 424	**TR**	P	*TR*	SU	77337	62914	71795	77336
319 425	**TR**	P	*TR*	SU	77339	62915	71796	77338
319 426	**TR**	P	*TR*	SU	77341	62916	71797	77340

319 427	**TR**	P	*TR*	SU	77343	62917	71798	77342
319 428	**TR**	P	*TR*	SU	77345	62918	71799	77344
319 429	**TR**	P	*TR*	SU	77347	62919	71800	77346
319 430	**TR**	P	*TR*	SU	77349	62920	71801	77348
319 431	**TR**	P	*TR*	SU	77351	62921	71802	77350
319 432	**TR**	P	*TR*	SU	77353	62922	71803	77352
319 433	**TR**	P	*TR*	SU	77355	62923	71804	77354
319 434	**TR**	P	*TR*	SU	77357	62924	71805	77356
319 435	**TR**	P	*TR*	SU	77359	62925	71806	77358
319 436	**TR**	P	*TR*	SU	77361	62926	71807	77360
319 437	**TR**	P	*TR*	SU	77363	62927	71808	77362
319 438	**TR**	P	*TR*	SU	77365	62928	71809	77364
319 439	**TR**	P	*TR*	SU	77367	62929	71810	77366
319 440	**TR**	P	*TR*	SU	77369	62930	71811	77368
319 441	**TR**	P	*TR*	SU	77371	62931	71812	77370
319 442	**TR**	P	*TR*	SU	77373	62932	71813	77372
319 443	**TR**	P	*TR*	SU	77375	62933	71814	77374
319 444	**TR**	P	*TR*	SU	77377	62934	71815	77376
319 445	**TR**	P	*TR*	SU	77379	62935	71816	77378
319 446	**TR**	P	*TR*	SU	77381	62936	71817	77380
319 447	**TR**	P	*TR*	SU	77431	62961	71866	77430
319 448	**TR**	P	*TR*	SU	77433	62962	71867	77432
319 449	**TR**	P	*TR*	SU	77435	62963	71868	77434
319 450	**TR**	P	*TR*	SU	77437	62964	71869	77436
319 451	**TR**	P	*TR*	SU	77439	62965	71870	77438
319 452	**TR**	P	*TR*	SU	77441	62966	71871	77440
319 453	**TR**	P	*TR*	SU	77443	62967	71872	77442
319 454	**TR**	P	*TR*	SU	77445	62968	71873	77444
319 455	**TR**	P	*TR*	SU	77447	62969	71874	77446
319 456	**TR**	P	*TR*	SU	77449	62970	71875	77448
319 457	**TR**	P	*TR*	SU	77451	62971	71876	77450
319 458	**TR**	P	*TR*	SU	77453	62972	71877	77452
319 459	**TR**	P	*TR*	SU	77455	62973	71878	77454
319 460	**TR**	P	*TR*	SU	77457	62974	71879	77456

CLASS 320   BREL YORK

ScotRail suburban units.
Formation: DTSO–MSO–DTSO.
Construction: Steel
Traction Motors: Four Brush TM2141B of 268 kW.
Doors: Sliding.   **Control System:** Thyristor.
Gangways: Within unit.   **Bogies:** P7-4 (MSO), T3-7 (others).
Couplers: Tightlock.   **Maximum Speed:** 75 m.p.h.
Seating Layout: 3+2 facing.   **Dimensions:** 20.18 x 2.82 m.
Braking: Disc.
Multiple Working: Within class and with Classes 317, 318, 319, 321, 322 and 323.

DTSO (A). Lot No. 31060 1990. –/76. 30.7 t.
MSO. Lot No. 31062 1990. –/76. 52.1 t.
DTSO (B). Lot No. 31061 1990. –/75 1W. 31.7 t.

320 301	**SC**	H	*SR*	GW	77899	63021	77921
320 302	**SC**	H	*SR*	GW	77900	63022	77922
320 303	**SC**	H	*SR*	GW	77901	63023	77923
320 304	**SC**	H	*SR*	GW	77902	63024	77924
320 305	**S**	H	*SR*	GW	77903	63025	77925
320 306	**SC**	H	*SR*	GW	77904	63026	77926
320 307	**SC**	H	*SR*	GW	77905	63027	77927
320 308	**SC**	H	*SR*	GW	77906	63028	77928
320 309	**SC**	H	*SR*	GW	77907	63029	77929
320 310	**SC**	H	*SR*	GW	77908	63030	77930
320 311	**SC**	H	*SR*	GW	77909	63031	77931
320 312	**SC**	H	*SR*	GW	77910	63032	77932
320 313	**SC**	H	*SR*	GW	77911	63033	77933
320 314	**SC**	H	*SR*	GW	77912	63034	77934
320 315	**SC**	H	*SR*	GW	77913	63035	77935
320 316	**SC**	H	*SR*	GW	77914	63036	77936
320 317	**SC**	H	*SR*	GW	77915	63037	77937
320 318	**SC**	H	*SR*	GW	77916	63038	77938
320 319	**SC**	H	*SR*	GW	77917	63039	77939
320 320	**SC**	H	*SR*	GW	77918	63040	77940
320 321	**SC**	H	*SR*	GW	77919	63041	77941
320 322	**SC**	H	*SR*	GW	77920	63042	77942

Names (carried on MSO):

320 305	GLASGOW SCHOOL OF ART 1844–150–1994
320 306	Model Rail Scotland
320 308	High Road 20th Anniversary 2000
320 309	Radio Clyde 25th Anniversary
320 311	Royal College of Physicians and Surgeons of Glasgow.
320 321	The Rt. Hon. John Smith, QC, MP
320 322	Festive Glasgow Orchid

CLASS 321   BREL YORK

Formation: DTCO (DTSO on Class 321/9)–MSO–TSO–DTSO.
Construction: Steel.
Traction Motors: Four Brush TM2141C (268 kW).
Doors: Sliding.   **Control System:** Thyristor.
Gangways: Within unit.   **Bogies:** P7-4 (MSO), T3-7 (others).
Couplers: Tightlock   **Maximum Speed:** 100 m.p.h.
Seating Layout: 1: 2+2 facing, 2: 3+2 facing.
Dimensions: 20.18 x 2.82 m.
Braking: Disc.
Multiple Working: Within class and with Classes 317, 318, 319, 320, 322 and 323.

Class 321/3. First Great Eastern units.

DTCO. Lot No. 31053 1988–1990. 16/57. 29.3 t.
MSO. Lot No. 31054 1988–1990. –/82. 51.5 t.
TSO. Lot No. 31055 1988–1990. –/75 2T. 28 t.
DTSO. Lot No. 31056 1988–1990. –/78. 29.1 t.

321 301	GE	H	GE	IL	78049	62975	71880	77853
321 302	GE	H	GE	IL	78050	62976	71881	77854
321 303	GE	H	GE	IL	78051	62977	71882	77855
321 304	GE	H	GE	IL	78052	62978	71883	77856
321 305	GE	H	GE	IL	78053	62979	71884	77857
321 306	GE	H	GE	IL	78054	62980	71885	77858
321 307	GE	H	GE	IL	78055	62981	71886	77859
321 308	GE	H	GE	IL	78056	62982	71887	77860
321 309	GE	H	GE	IL	78057	62983	71888	77861
321 310	GE	H	GE	IL	78058	62984	71889	77862
321 311	GE	H	GE	IL	78059	62985	71890	77863
321 312	GE	H	GE	IL	78060	62986	71891	77864
321 313	GE	H	GE	IL	78061	62987	71892	77865
321 314	GE	H	GE	IL	78062	62988	71893	77866
321 315	GE	H	GE	IL	78063	62989	71894	77867
321 316	GE	H	GE	IL	78064	62990	71895	77868
321 317	GE	H	GE	IL	78065	62991	71896	77869
321 318	GE	H	GE	IL	78066	62992	71897	77870
321 319	GE	H	GE	IL	78067	62993	71898	77871
321 320	GE	H	GE	IL	78068	62994	71899	77872
321 321	GE	H	GE	IL	78069	62995	71900	77873
321 322	GE	H	GE	IL	78070	62996	71901	77874
321 323	GE	H	GE	IL	78071	62997	71902	77875
321 324	GE	H	GE	IL	78072	62998	71903	77876
321 325	GE	H	GE	IL	78073	62999	71904	77877
321 326	GE	H	GE	IL	78074	63000	71905	77878
321 327	GE	H	GE	IL	78075	63001	71906	77879
321 328	GE	H	GE	IL	78076	63002	71907	77880
321 329	GE	H	GE	IL	78077	63003	71908	77881
321 330	GE	H	GE	IL	78078	63004	71909	77882
321 331	GE	H	GE	IL	78079	63005	71910	77883
321 332	GE	H	GE	IL	78080	63006	71911	77884
321 333	GE	H	GE	IL	78081	63007	71912	77885
321 334	GE	H	GE	IL	78082	63008	71913	77886
321 335	GE	H	GE	IL	78083	63009	71914	77887
321 336	GE	H	GE	IL	78084	63010	71915	77888
321 337	GE	H	GE	IL	78085	63011	71916	77889
321 338	GE	H	GE	IL	78086	63012	71917	77890
321 339	GE	H	GE	IL	78087	63013	71918	77891
321 340	GE	H	GE	IL	78088	63014	71919	77892
321 341	GE	H	GE	IL	78089	63015	71920	77893
321 342	GE	H	GE	IL	78090	63016	71921	77894
321 343	GE	H	GE	IL	78091	63017	71922	77895
321 344	GE	H	GE	IL	78092	63018	71923	77896
321 345	GE	H	GE	IL	78093	63019	71924	77897
321 346	GE	H	GE	IL	78094	63020	71925	77898
321 347	GE	H	GE	IL	78131	63105	71991	78280
321 348	GE	H	GE	IL	78132	63106	71992	78281
321 349	GE	H	GE	IL	78133	63107	71993	78282
321 350	GE	H	GE	IL	78134	63108	71994	78283
321 351	GE	H	GE	IL	78135	63109	71995	78284

321 352	**GE**	H	*GE*	IL	78136	63110	71996	78285
321 353	**GE**	H	*GE*	IL	78137	63111	71997	78286
321 354	**GE**	H	*GE*	IL	78138	63112	71998	78287
321 355	**GE**	H	*GE*	IL	78139	63113	71999	78288
321 356	**GE**	H	*GE*	IL	78140	63114	72000	78289
321 357	**GE**	H	*GE*	IL	78141	63115	72001	78290
321 358	**GE**	H	*GE*	IL	78142	63116	72002	78291
321 359	**GE**	H	*GE*	IL	78143	63117	72003	78292
321 360	**GE**	H	*GE*	IL	78144	63118	72004	78293
321 361	**GE**	H	*GE*	IL	78145	63119	72005	78294
321 362	**GE**	H	*GE*	IL	78146	63120	72006	78295
321 363	**GE**	H	*GE*	IL	78147	63121	72007	78296
321 364	**GE**	H	*GE*	IL	78148	63122	72008	78297
321 365	**GE**	H	*GE*	IL	78149	63123	72009	78298
321 366	**GE**	H	*GE*	IL	78150	63124	72010	78299

Names (carried on TSO):

321 312	Southend-on-Sea
321 321	NSPCC ESSEX FULL STOP
321 336	GEOFFREY FREEMAN ALLEN
321 334	Amsterdam
321 343	RSA–RAILWAY STUDY ASSOCIATION
321 351	GURKHA

Class 321/4. Silverlink/First Great Eastern units.

DTCO. Lot No. 31067 1989–1990. 28/40. 29.3 t.
MSO. Lot No. 31068 1989–1990. –/79. 51.5 t.
TSO. Lot No. 31069 1989–1990. –/74 2T. 28 t.
DTSO. Lot No. 31070 1989–1990. –/78. 29.1 t.

Note: The DTCOs of FGE units have had 12 first class seats declassified.

321 401	**SL**	H	*SL*	BY	78095	63063	71949	77943
321 402	**SL**	H	*SL*	BY	78096	63064	71950	77944
321 403	**SL**	H	*SL*	BY	78097	63065	71951	77945
321 404	**SL**	H	*SL*	BY	78098	63066	71952	77946
321 405	**SL**	H	*SL*	BY	78099	63067	71953	77947
321 406	**SL**	H	*SL*	BY	78100	63068	71954	77948
321 407	**SL**	H	*SL*	BY	78101	63069	71955	77949
321 408	**SL**	H	*SL*	BY	78102	63070	71956	77950
321 409	**SL**	H	*SL*	BY	78103	63071	71957	77951
321 410	**SL**	H	*SL*	BY	78104	63072	71958	77952
321 411	**SL**	H	*SL*	BY	78105	63073	71959	77953
321 412	**SL**	H	*SL*	BY	78106	63074	71960	77954
321 413	**SL**	H	*SL*	BY	78107	63075	71961	77955
321 414	**SL**	H	*SL*	BY	78108	63076	71962	77956
321 415	**SL**	H	*SL*	BY	78109	63077	71963	77957
321 416	**SL**	H	*SL*	BY	78110	63078	71964	77958
321 417	**SL**	H	*SL*	BY	78111	63079	71965	77959
321 418	**SL**	H	*SL*	BY	78112	63080	71968	77962
321 419	**SL**	H	*SL*	BY	78113	63081	71967	77961
321 420	**SL**	H	*SL*	BY	78114	63082	71966	77960

321 421	**SL**	H	*SL*	BY	78115	63083	71969	77963
321 422	**SL**	H	*SL*	BY	78116	63084	71970	77964
321 423	**SL**	H	*SL*	BY	78117	63085	71971	77965
321 424	**SL**	H	*SL*	BY	78118	63086	71972	77966
321 425	**N**	H	*SL*	BY	78119	63087	71973	77967
321 426	**SL**	H	*SL*	BY	78120	63088	71974	77968
321 427	**SL**	H	*SL*	BY	78121	63089	71975	77969
321 428	**SL**	H	*SL*	BY	78122	63090	71976	77970
321 429	**SL**	H	*SL*	BY	78123	63091	71977	77971
321 430	**SL**	H	*SL*	BY	78124	63092	71978	77972
321 431	**SL**	H	*SL*	BY	78151	63125	72011	78300
321 432	**SL**	H	*SL*	BY	78152	63126	72012	78301
321 433	**SL**	H	*SL*	BY	78153	63127	72013	78302
321 434	**SL**	H	*SL*	BY	78154	63128	72014	70303
321 435	**SL**	H	*SL*	BY	78155	63129	72015	78304
321 436	**SL**	H	*SL*	BY	78156	63130	72016	78305
321 437	**SL**	H	*SL*	BY	78157	63131	72017	78306
321 438	**GE**	H	*GE*	IL	78158	63132	72018	78307
321 439	**GE**	H	*GE*	IL	78159	63133	72019	78308
321 440	**GE**	H	*GE*	IL	78160	63134	72020	78309
321 441	**GE**	H	*GE*	IL	78161	63135	72021	78310
321 442	**GE**	H	*GE*	IL	78162	63136	72022	78311
321 443	**GE**	H	*GE*	IL	78125	63099	71985	78274
321 444	**GE**	H	*GE*	IL	78126	63100	71986	78275
321 445	**GE**	H	*GE*	IL	78127	63101	71987	78276
321 446	**GE**	H	*GE*	IL	78128	63102	71988	78277
321 447	**GE**	H	*GE*	IL	78129	63103	71989	78278
321 448	**GE**	H	*GE*	IL	78130	63104	71990	78279

Names (carried on TSO):

321 407	HERTFORDSHIRE WRVS
321 413	Bill Green
321 427	Major Tim Warr
321 439	Chelmsford Cathedral Festival
321 444	Essex Lifeboats

Class 321/9. DTSO(A)–MSO–TSO–DTSO(B). Units leased by West Yorkshire PTE from International Bank of Scotland. Managed by Porterbrook Leasing Company.

DTSO(A). Lot No. 31108 1991. –/77. 29.3 t.
MSO. Lot No. 31109 1991. –/79. 51.5 t.
TSO. Lot No. 31110 1991. –/74 2T. 28 t.
DTSO(B). Dia. EE277. Lot No. 31111 1991. –/77. 29.1 t.

321 901	**WY**	P	*AN*	NL	77991	63153	72128	77993
321 902	**WY**	P	*AN*	NL	77990	63154	72129	77994
321 903	**WY**	P	*AN*	NL	77992	63155	72130	77995

CLASS 322   BREL YORK

Units built for use on Stansted Airport services. Now working on ScotRail on the
Edinburgh–North Berwick line.

Formation: DTCO (declassified)–MSO–TSO–DTSO.
Construction: Steel.
Traction Motors: Four Brush TM2141C (268 kW).
Doors: Sliding.   **Control System:** Thyristor.
Gangways: Within unit.   **Bogies:** P7-4 (MSO), T3-7 (others).
Couplers: Tightlock   **Maximum Speed:** 100 m.p.h.
Seating Layout: 1: 2+1 facing, 2: 2+2 facing.
Dimensions: 20.18 x 2.82 m.
Braking: Disc.
Multiple Working: Within class and with Classes 317, 318, 319, 320, 321 and 323.

DTCO. Lot No. 31094 1990. 35/22. 30.4 t.
MSO. Lot No. 31092 1990. –/70. 52.3 t.
TSO. Lot No. 31093 1990. –/60 2T. 29.5 t.
DTSO. Lot No. 31091 1990. –/65. 29.8 t.

Non-Standard livery: Stansted Skytrain livery (light grey with a yellow stripe,
now also with ScotRail brandings).

322 481	**0**	H	*SR*	GW	78163	72023	63137	77985
322 482	**0**	H	*SR*	GW	78164	72024	63138	77986
322 483	**0**	H	*SR*	GW	78165	72025	63139	77987
322 484	**NW**	H	*SR*	GW	78166	72026	63140	77988
322 485	**0**	H	*SR*	GW	78167	72027	63141	77989

Name (carried on MSO):

322 485   North Berwick Flyer 1850–2000.

CLASS 323 HUNSLET TRANSPORTATION PROJECTS

Birmingham and Greater Manchester area suburban units.
Formation: DMSO(A)–PTSO–DMSO(B).
Construction: Welded aluminium alloy.
Doors: Sliding plug.
Traction Motors: Four Holec DMKT 52/24 of 146 kW.
Gangways: Within unit.
Bogies: SRP BP62 (DMSO), BT52 (PTSO).
Couplers: Tightlock   **Maximum Speed:** 100 m.p.h.
Seating Layout: 3+2 facing/unidirectional.
Dimensions: 23.27/23.44 x 2.80 m.
Braking: Disc.
Multiple Working: Within class and with Classes 317, 318, 319, 320, 321 and 322.

DMSO(A). Lot No. 31112 Hunslet 1992–1993. –/98 (* –/82). 41.0 t.
TSO. Lot No. 31113 Hunslet 1992–1993. –/88 1T. (* –/80 1T). 23.37 t.
DMSO(B). Lot No. 31114 Hunslet 1992–1993. –/98 (* –/82). 39.4 t.

323 201		CO	P	*CT*	SI	64001	72201	65001
323 202		CO	P	*CT*	SI	64002	72202	65002
323 203		CO	P	*CT*	SI	64003	72203	65003
323 204		CO	P	*CT*	SI	64004	72204	65004
323 205		CO	P	*CT*	SI	64005	72205	65005
323 206		CO	P	*CT*	SI	64006	72206	65006
323 207		CO	P	*CT*	SI	64007	72207	65007
323 208		CO	P	*CT*	SI	64008	72208	65008
323 209		CO	P	*CT*	SI	64009	72209	65009
323 210		CO	P	*CT*	SI	64010	72210	65010
323 211		CO	P	*CT*	SI	64011	72211	65011
323 212		CO	P	*CT*	SI	64012	72212	65012
323 213		CO	P	*CT*	SI	64013	72213	65013
323 214		CO	P	*CT*	SI	64014	72214	65014
323 215		CO	P	*CT*	SI	64015	72215	65015
323 216		CO	P	*CT*	SI	64016	72216	65016
323 217		CO	P	*CT*	SI	64017	72217	65017
323 218		CO	P	*CT*	SI	64018	72218	65018
323 219		CO	P	*CT*	SI	64019	72219	65019
323 220		CO	P	*CT*	SI	64020	72220	65020
323 221		CO	P	*CT*	SI	64021	72221	65021
323 222		CO	P	*CT*	SI	64022	72222	65022
323 223	*	GM	P	*NW*	LG	64023	72223	65023
323 224	*	NW	P	*NW*	LG	64024	72224	65024
323 225	*	GM	P	*NW*	LG	64025	72225	65025
323 226		FS	P	*NW*	LG	64026	72226	65026
323 227		FS	P	*NW*	LG	64027	72227	65027
323 228		FS	P	*NW*	LG	64028	72228	65028
323 229		FS	P	*NW*	LG	64029	72229	65029
323 230		FS	P	*NW*	LG	64030	72230	65030
323 231		FS	P	*NW*	LG	64031	72231	65031
323 232		FS	P	*NW*	LG	64032	72232	65032
323 233		FS	P	*NW*	LG	64033	72233	65033
323 234		FS	P	*NW*	LG	64034	72234	65034
323 235		FS	P	*NW*	LG	64035	72235	65035
323 236		FS	P	*NW*	LG	64036	72236	65036
323 237		GM	P	*NW*	LG	64037	72237	65037
323 238		GM	P	*NW*	LG	64038	72238	65038
323 239		FS	P	*NW*	LG	64039	72239	65039
323 240		CO	P	*CT*	SI	64040	72340	65040
323 241		CO	P	*CT*	SI	64041	72341	65041
323 242		CO	P	*CT*	SI	64042	72342	65042
323 243		CO	P	*CT*	SI	64043	72343	65043

CLASS 325   ABB DERBY

Postal units based on Class 319. Compatible with diesel locomotive haulage.
Formation: DTPMV–MPMV–TPMV–DTPMV.
System: 25 kV AC overhead/750 V DC third rail.
Construction: Steel.
Traction Motors: Four GEC G315BZ of 268 kW.

Doors: Roller shutter.
Gangways: None.
Couplers: Drop-head buckeye.
Braking: Disc.
Multiple Working: Within class.

Control System: GTO chopper.
Bogies: P7-4 (MSO), T3-7 (others).
Maximum Speed: 100 m.p.h.
Dimensions: 20.18 x 2.82 m.

DTPMV. Lot No. 31144 1995.
MPMV. Lot No. 31145 1995.
TPMV. Lot No. 31146 1995.

325 001	**RM**	RM *E*	CE	68300	68340	68360	68301
325 002	**RM**	RM *E*	CE	68302	68341	68361	68303
325 003	**RM**	RM *E*	CE	68304	68342	68362	68305
325 004	**RM**	RM *E*	CE	68306	68343	68363	68307
325 005	**RM**	RM *E*	CE	68308	68344	68364	68309
325 006	**RM**	RM *E*	CE	68310	68345	68365	68311
325 007	**RM**	RM *E*	CE	68312	68346	68366	68313
325 008	**RM**	RM *E*	CE	68314	68347	68367	68315
325 009	**RM**	RM *E*	CE	68316	68348	68368	68317
325 010	**RM**	RM *E*	CE	68318	68349	68369	68319
325 011	**RM**	RM *E*	CE	68320	68350	68370	68321
325 012	**RM**	RM *E*	CE	68322	68351	68371	68323
325 013	**RM**	RM *E*	CE	68324	68352	68372	68325
325 014	**RM**	RM *E*	CE	68326	68353	68373	68327
325 015	**RM**	RM *E*	CE	68328	68354	68374	68329
325 016	**RM**	RM *E*	CE	68330	68355	68375	68331

Names (carried on one side of each DTPMV):

325 002   Royal Mail North Wales & North West
325 006   John Grierson
325 008   Peter Howarth C.B.E.

CLASS 332   HEATHROW EXPRESS   SIEMENS

Dedicated Heathrow Express units. Five units were increased from 4-car to 5-car in 2002. Usually operate in coupled pairs.
Formations: Various.
Construction: Steel.
Traction Motors: Two Siemens monomotors of 350 kW.
Gangways: Within unit.
Couplers: Scharfenberg
Seating Layout: 1: 2+1 facing, 2: 2+2 mainly unidirectional.
Dimensions: 23.74/23.15 x 2.80 m.
Multiple Working: Within class and with Class 333.

Doors: Sliding plug.

Bogies: CAF.
Maximum Speed: 100 m.p.h.

Braking: Disc.

332 001–332 007. DMFO–TSO–PTSO–(TSO)–DMSO.

DMFO. CAF 1997–1998. 26/–. 48.8 t.
TSO. CAF 1997–1998. –/56 35.8 t.
PTSO. CAF 1997–1998. –/44 1TD 1W. 45.6 t.
TSO. CAF 2002. –/56 35.8 t. (new TSOs fitted to 332 005–332 007).
DMSO. CAF 1997–1998. –/48. 48.8 t.

Advertising livery: Vehicles 78401, 78402, 78405, 78406, 78408, 78410, 78412 carry Royal Bank of Scotland advertising livery (deep blue).

332 001	**HE**	HE *HE*	OH	78400	72412	63400		78401
332 002	**HE**	HE *HE*	OH	78402	72409	63401		78403
332 003	**HE**	HE *HE*	OH	78404	72407	63402		78405
332 004	**HE**	HE *HE*	OH	78406	72405	63403		78407
332 005	**HE**	HE *HE*	OH	78408	72411	63404	72417	78409
332 006	**HE**	HE *HE*	OH	78410	72410	63405	72415	78411
332 007	**HE**	HE *HE*	OH	78412	72401	63406	72414	78413

332 008–332 014. DMSO–TSO–PTSO–(TSO)–DMLFO.

DMSO. CAF 1997–1998. –/48. 48.8 t.
TSO. CAF 1997–1998. –/56 35.8 t.
PTSO. CAF 1997–1998. –/44 1TD 1W. 45.6 t.
TSO. CAF 2002. –/56 35.8 t. (new TSOs fitted to 332 008–332 009).
DMLFO. CAF 1997–1998. 14/– 1W. 48.8 t.

Advertising livery: Vehicles 78414, 78416, 78419, 78421, 78423, 78425, 78427 carry Royal Bank of Scotland advertising livery.

332 008	**HE**	HE *HE*	OH	78414	72413	63407	72418	78415
332 009	**HE**	HE *HE*	OH	78416	72400	63408	72416	78417
332 010	**HE**	HE *HE*	OH	78418	72402	63409		78419
332 011	**HE**	HE *HE*	OH	78420	72403	63410		78421
332 012	**HE**	HE *HE*	OH	78422	72404	63411		78423
332 013	**HE**	HE *HE*	OH	78424	72408	63412		78425
332 014	**HE**	HE *HE*	OH	78426	72406	63413		78427

CLASS 333   SIEMENS

Formation: DMSO–PTSO–TSO–DMSO.
Construction: Steel.   **Doors**: Sliding plug.
Traction Motors: Two Siemens monomotors of 350 kW.
Gangways: Within unit.   **Bogies**: CAF.
Couplers: Scharfenberg   **Maximum Speed**: 100 m.p.h.
Seating Layout: 3+2 facing/unidirectional.
Dimensions: 23.74/23.15 x 2.80 m.   **Braking**: Disc.
Multiple Working: Within class and with Class 332.

DMSO(A). (Odd Nos.) CAF 2001. –/90. 50.0 t.
PTSO. CAF 2001. –/73 1TD 2W. 46.0 t.
TSO. CAF 2002–2003. –/100. 37.0 t.
DMSO(B). (Even Nos.) CAF 2001. –/90. 50.0 t.

Note: 333 001–333 008 were made up to 4-car units from 3-car units in 2002. 333 009–333 016 were made up to 4-car units from 3-car units in 2003.

333 001	**YN**	A	*AN*	NL	78451	74461	74477	78452
333 002	**YN**	A	*AN*	NL	78453	74462	74478	78454
333 003	**YN**	A	*AN*	NL	78455	74463	74479	78456
333 004	**YN**	A	*AN*	NL	78457	74464	74480	78458
333 005	**YN**	A	*AN*	NL	78459	74465	74481	78460
333 006	**YN**	A	*AN*	NL	78461	74466	74482	78462

333 007	**YN**	A	*AN*	NL	78463	74467	74483	78464
333 008	**YN**	A	*AN*	NL	78465	74468	74484	78466
333 009	**YN**	A	*AN*	NL	78467	74469	74485	78468
333 010	**YN**	A	*AN*	NL	78469	74470	74486	78470
333 011	**YN**	A	*AN*	NL	78471	74471	74487	78472
333 012	**YN**	A	*AN*	NL	78473	74472	74488	78474
333 013	**YN**	A	*AN*	NL	78475	74473	74489	78476
333 014	**YN**	A	*AN*	NL	78477	74474	74490	78478
333 015	**YN**	A	*AN*	NL	78479	74475	74491	78480
333 016	**YN**	A	*AN*	NL	78481	74476	74492	78482

CLASS 334 JUNIPER ALSTOM BIRMINGHAM

ScotRail outer suburban units.
Formations: DMSO–PTSO–DMSO.
Construction: Steel.   **Doors:** Sliding plug.
Traction Motors: Two Alstom ONIX 800 of 270 kW.
Gangways: Within unit.   **Bogies:** Alstom LTB3/TBP3.
Couplers: Tightlock.   **Maximum Speed:** 100 m.p.h.
Seating Layout: 2+2 facing/unidirectional (3+2 in PTSO).
Dimensions: 21.16/19.94 x 2.80 m.   **Braking:** Disc.
Multiple Working: Within class.

64101–64140. DMSO. Alstom Birmingham 1999–2001. –/64. 42.6 t.
PTSO. Alstom Birmingham 1999–2001. –/55 1TD 1W. 39.4 t.
65101–65140. DMSO. Alstom Birmingham 1999–2001. –/64. 42.6 t.

334 001	**SP**	H	*SR*	GW	64101	74301	65101
334 002	**SP**	H	*SR*	GW	64102	74302	65102
334 003	**SP**	H	*SR*	GW	64103	74303	65103
334 004	**SP**	H	*SR*	GW	64104	74304	65104
334 005	**SP**	H	*SR*	GW	64105	74305	65105
334 006	**SP**	H	*SR*	GW	64106	74306	65106
334 007	**SP**	H	*SR*	GW	64107	74307	65107
334 008	**SP**	H	*SR*	GW	64108	74308	65108
334 009	**SP**	H	*SR*	GW	64109	74309	65109
334 010	**SP**	H	*SR*	GW	64110	74310	65110
334 011	**SP**	H	*SR*	GW	64111	74311	65111
334 012	**SP**	H	*SR*	GW	64112	74312	65112
334 013	**SP**	H	*SR*	GW	64113	74313	65113
334 014	**SP**	H	*SR*	GW	64114	74314	65114
334 015	**SP**	H	*SR*	GW	64115	74315	65115
334 016	**SP**	H	*SR*	GW	64116	74316	65116
334 017	**SP**	H	*SR*	GW	64117	74317	65117
334 018	**SP**	H	*SR*	GW	64118	74318	65118
334 019	**SP**	H	*SR*	GW	64119	74319	65119
334 020	**SP**	H	*SR*	GW	64120	74320	65120
334 021	**SP**	H	*SR*	GW	64121	74321	65121
334 022	**SP**	H	*SR*	GW	64122	74322	65122
334 023	**SP**	H	*SR*	GW	64123	74323	65123
334 024	**SP**	H	*SR*	GW	64124	74324	65124
334 025	**SP**	H	*SR*	GW	64125	74325	65125

334 026	**SP**	H	*SR*	GW	64126	74326	65126
334 027	**SP**	H	*SR*	GW	64127	74327	65127
334 028	**SP**	H	*SR*	GW	64128	74328	65128
334 029	**SP**	H	*SR*	GW	64129	74329	65129
334 030	**SP**	H	*SR*	GW	64130	74330	65130
334 031	**SP**	H	*SR*	GW	64131	74331	65131
334 032	**SP**	H	*SR*	GW	64132	74332	65132
334 033	**SP**	H	*SR*	GW	64133	74333	65133
334 034	**SP**	H	*SR*	GW	64134	74334	65134
334 035	**SP**	H	*SR*	GW	64135	74335	65135
334 036	**SP**	H	*SR*	GW	64136	74336	65136
334 037	**SP**	H	*SR*	GW	64137	74337	65137
334 038	**SP**	H	*SR*	GW	64138	74338	65138
334 039	**SP**	H	*SR*	GW	64139	74339	65139
334 040	**SP**	H	*SR*	GW	64140	74340	65140

Name:

334 001   Donald Dewar.

CLASS 350/1   DESIRO UK   SIEMENS

New units on order for Angel Trains.
Formation: DMCO(A)–PTSO–TSO–DMCO(B).
Systems: 25 kV AC overhead.
Construction: Welded aluminium.   **Doors**: Sliding plug.
Traction Motors: 4 Siemens 1TB2016-0GB02 asynchronous of 250 kW.
Gangways: Within unit only.   **Bogies**: SGP SF5000.
Couplers: Dellner 12.   **Maximum Speed**: 100 m.p.h.
Seating Layout: 1: 2+1 facing, 2: 2+2.
Dimensions: 20.40 x 2.79 m.   **Multiple Working**: Within class.
Braking: Disc & regenerative.

DMCO(A). Siemens Uerdingen 2004–05.
PTSO. Siemens Wien 2004–05.
TSO. Siemens Wien 2004–05.
DMCO(B). Siemens Uerdingen 2004–05.

350 101	A	63761	66811	66861	63711
350 102	A	63762	66812	66862	63712
350 103	A	63763	66813	66863	63713
350 104	A	63764	66814	66864	63714
350 105	A	63765	66815	66865	63715
350 106	A	63766	66816	66866	63716
350 107	A	63767	66817	66867	63717
350 108	A	63768	66818	66868	63718
350 109	A	63769	66819	66869	63719
350 110	A	63770	66820	66870	63720
350 111	A	63771	66821	66871	63721
350 112	A	63772	66822	66872	63722
350 113	A	63773	66823	66873	63723
350 114	A	63774	66824	66874	63724
350 115	A	63775	66825	66875	63725

350 116	A		63776	66826	66876	63726
350 117	A		63777	66827	66877	63727
350 118	A		63778	66828	66878	63728
350 119	A		63779	66829	66879	63729
350 120	A		63780	66830	66880	63730
350 121	A		63781	66831	66881	63731
350 122	A		63782	66832	66882	63732
350 123	A		63783	66833	66883	63733
350 124	A		63784	66834	66884	63734
350 125	A		63785	66835	66885	63735
350 126	A		63786	66836	66886	63736
350 127	A		63787	66837	66887	63737
350 128	A		63788	66838	66888	63738
350 129	A		63789	66839	66889	63739
350 130	A		63790	66840	66890	63740

CLASS 357 ELECTROSTAR
ADTRANZ/BOMBARDIER DERBY

c2c units. Provision for 750 V DC supply if required.

Formation: DMSO(A)–MSO–PTSO–DMSO(B).
Construction: Welded aluminium alloy underframe, sides and roof with steel ends. All sections bolted together.
Traction Motors: Two Adtranz 250 kW.
Doors: Sliding plug.
Gangways: Within unit.   **Bogies:** Adtranz P3-25/T3-25.
Couplers: Tightlock.   **Maximum Speed:** 100 m.p.h.
Seating Layout: 3+2 facing/unidirectional.
Dimensions: 20.40/19.99 x 2.80 m.
Braking: Disc & regenerative.   **Multiple Working:** Within class.

Class 357/0. Owned by Porterbrook Leasing.

DMSO(A). Adtranz Derby 1999–2001. –/71. 40.7 t.
MSO. Adtranz Derby 1999–2001. –/78. 39.5 t.
PTSO. Adtranz Derby 1999–2001. –/62 1TD 2W. 36.7 t.
DMSO(B). Adtranz Derby 1999–2001. –/71. 40.7 t.

357 001	**C2**	P	*C2*	EM	67651	74151	74051	67751
357 002	**C2**	P	*C2*	EM	67652	74152	74052	67752
357 003	**C2**	P	*C2*	EM	67653	74153	74053	67753
357 004	**C2**	P	*C2*	EM	67654	74154	74054	67754
357 005	**C2**	P	*C2*	EM	67655	74155	74055	67755
357 006	**C2**	P	*C2*	EM	67656	74156	74056	67756
357 007	**C2**	P	*C2*	EM	67657	74157	74057	67757
357 008	**C2**	P	*C2*	EM	67658	74158	74058	67758
357 009	**C2**	P	*C2*	EM	67659	74159	74059	67759
357 010	**C2**	P	*C2*	EM	67660	74160	74060	67760
357 011	**C2**	P	*C2*	EM	67661	74161	74061	67761
357 012	**C2**	P	*C2*	EM	67662	74162	74062	67762
357 013	**C2**	P	*C2*	EM	67663	74163	74063	67763

357 014	**C2**	P	*C2*	EM	67664	74164	74064	67764
357 015	**C2**	P	*C2*	EM	67665	74165	74065	67765
357 016	**C2**	P	*C2*	EM	67666	74166	74066	67766
357 017	**C2**	P	*C2*	EM	67667	74167	74067	67767
357 018	**C2**	P	*C2*	EM	67668	74168	74068	67768
357 019	**C2**	P	*C2*	EM	67669	74169	74069	67769
357 020	**C2**	P	*C2*	EM	67670	74170	74070	67770
357 021	**C2**	P	*C2*	EM	67671	74171	74071	67771
357 022	**C2**	P	*C2*	EM	67672	74172	74072	67772
357 023	**C2**	P	*C2*	EM	67673	74173	74073	67773
357 024	**C2**	P	*C2*	EM	67674	74174	74074	67774
357 025	**C2**	P	*C2*	EM	67675	74175	74075	67775
357 026	**C2**	P	*C2*	EM	67676	74176	74076	67776
357 027	**C2**	P	*C2*	EM	67677	74177	74077	67777
357 028	**C2**	P	*C2*	EM	67678	74178	74078	67778
357 029	**C2**	P	*C2*	EM	67679	74179	74079	67779
357 030	**C2**	P	*C2*	EM	67680	74180	74080	67780
357 031	**C2**	P	*C2*	EM	67681	74181	74081	67781
357 032	**C2**	P	*C2*	EM	67682	74182	74082	67782
357 033	**C2**	P	*C2*	EM	67683	74183	74083	67783
357 034	**C2**	P	*C2*	EM	67684	74184	74084	67784
357 035	**C2**	P	*C2*	EM	67685	74185	74085	67785
357 036	**C2**	P	*C2*	EM	67686	74186	74086	67786
357 037	**C2**	P	*C2*	EM	67687	74187	74087	67787
357 038	**C2**	P	*C2*	EM	67688	74188	74088	67788
357 039	**C2**	P	*C2*	EM	67689	74189	74089	67789
357 040	**C2**	P	*C2*	EM	67690	74190	74090	67790
357 041	**C2**	P	*C2*	EM	67691	74191	74091	67791
357 042	**C2**	P	*C2*	EM	67692	74192	74092	67792
357 043	**C2**	P	*C2*	EM	67693	74193	74093	67793
357 044	**C2**	P	*C2*	EM	67694	74194	74094	67794
357 045	**C2**	P	*C2*	EM	67695	74195	74095	67795
357 046	**C2**	P	*C2*	EM	67696	74196	74096	67796

Class 357/2. Owned by Angel Trains.

DMSO(A). Bombardier Derby 2001–2002. –/71. 40.7 t.
MSO. Bombardier Derby 2001–2002. –/78. 39.5 t.
PTSO. Bombardier Derby 2001–2002. –/62 1TD 2W. 36.7 t.
DMSO(B). Bombardier Derby 2001–2002. –/71. 40.7 t.

357 201	**C2**	A	*C2*	EM	68601	74701	74601	68701
357 202	**C2**	A	*C2*	EM	68602	74702	74602	68702
357 203	**C2**	A	*C2*	EM	68603	74703	74603	68703
357 204	**C2**	A	*C2*	EM	68604	74704	74604	68704
357 205	**C2**	A	*C2*	EM	68605	74705	74605	68705
357 206	**C2**	A	*C2*	EM	68606	74706	74606	68706
357 207	**C2**	A	*C2*	EM	68607	74707	74607	68707
357 208	**C2**	A	*C2*	EM	68608	74708	74608	68708
357 209	**C2**	A	*C2*	EM	68609	74709	74609	68709
357 210	**C2**	A	*C2*	EM	68610	74710	74610	68710
357 211	**C2**	A	*C2*	EM	68611	74711	74611	68711

357 212	**C2**	A	*C2*	EM	68612	74712	74612	68712
357 213	**C2**	A	*C2*	EM	68613	74713	74613	68713
357 214	**C2**	A	*C2*	EM	68614	74714	74614	68714
357 215	**C2**	A	*C2*	EM	68615	74715	74615	68715
357 216	**C2**	A	*C2*	EM	68616	74716	74616	68716
357 217	**C2**	A	*C2*	EM	68617	74717	74617	68717
357 218	**C2**	A	*C2*	EM	68618	74718	74618	68718
357 219	**C2**	A	*C2*	EM	68619	74719	74619	68719
357 220	**C2**	A	*C2*	EM	68620	74720	74620	68720
357 221	**C2**	A	*C2*	EM	68621	74721	74621	68721
357 222	**C2**	A	*C2*	EM	68622	74722	74622	68722
357 223	**C2**	A	*C2*	EM	68623	74723	74623	68723
357 224	**C2**	A	*C2*	EM	68624	74724	74624	68724
357 225	**C2**	A	*C2*	EM	68625	74725	74625	68725
357 226	**C2**	A	*C2*	EM	68626	74726	74626	68726
357 227	**C2**	A	*C2*	EM	68627	74727	74627	68727
357 228	**C2**	A	*C2*	EM	68628	74728	74628	68728

Names (carried on DMSO(A) and DMSO(B) (one plate on each)):

357 201	KEN BIRD
357 202	KENNY MITCHELL
357 203	HENRY PUMFRETT

CLASS 360   DESIRO UK   SIEMENS

New First Great Eastern units.
Formation: DMCO(A)–PTSO–TSO–DMCO(B).
Systems: 25 kV AC overhead.
Construction: Welded aluminium.   **Doors:** Sliding plug.
Traction Motors: 4 Siemens 1TB2016-0GB02 asynchronous of 250 kW.
Gangways: Within unit only.   **Bogies:** SGP SF5000.
Couplers: Dellner 12.   **Maximum Speed:** 100 m.p.h.
Seating Layout: 1: 2+2 facing, 2: 3+2 facing/unidirectional.
Dimensions: 20.40 x 2.79 m.   **Multiple Working:** Within class.
Braking: Disc & regenerative.

DMCO(A). Siemens Uerdingen 2002–2003. 8/59. 45.0 t.
PTSO. Siemens Wien 2002–2003. –/69 1TD 2W. 43.0 t.
TSO. Siemens Wien 2002–2003. –/78. 35.0 t.
DMCO(B). Siemens Uerdingen 2002–2003. 8/59. 45.0 t.

360 101	**FS**	A	*GE*	IL	65551	72551	74551	68551
360 102	**FS**	A	*GE*	IL	65552	72552	74552	68552
360 103	**FS**	A	*GE*	IL	65553	72553	74553	68553
360 104	**FS**	A	*GE*	IL	65554	72554	74554	68554
360 105	**FS**	A	*GE*	IL	65555	72555	74555	68555
360 106	**FS**	A	*GE*	IL	65556	72556	74556	68556
360 107	**FS**	A	*GE*	IL	65557	72557	74557	68557
360 108	**FS**	A	*GE*	IL	65558	72558	74558	68558
360 109	**FS**	A	*GE*	IL	65559	72559	74559	68559
360 110	**FS**	A	*GE*	IL	65560	72560	74560	68560

360 111	FS	A	*GE*	IL	65561	72561	74561	68561
360 112	FS	A	*GE*	IL	65562	72562	74562	68562
360 113	FS	A	*GE*	IL	65563	72563	74563	68563
360 114	FS	A	*GE*	IL	65564	72564	74564	68564
360 115	FS	A			65565	72565	74565	68565
360 116	FS	A	*GE*	IL	65566	72566	74566	68566
360 117	FS	A	*GE*	IL	65567	72567	74567	68567
360 118	FS	A	*GE*	IL	65568	72568	74568	68568
360 119	FS	A	*GE*	IL	65569	72569	74569	68569
360 120	FS	A	*GE*	IL	65570	72570	74570	68570
360 121	FS	A	*GE*	IL	65571	72571	74571	68571

CLASS 365 NETWORKER EXPRESS ABB YORK

Formation: DMCO(A)–TSO–PTSO–DMCO(B).
Systems: 25 kV AC overhead/750 V DC third rail. WAGN units have no shoegear, i.e. 750 V DC cannot be used, whilst South Eastern Trains units have their pantograph apertures covered over so that the 25 kV AC system cannot be used.
Construction: Welded aluminium alloy.
Traction Motors: Four GEC-Alsthom G354CX 157 kW.
Doors: Sliding plug.
Gangways: Within unit.   **Bogies:** ABB P3-16/T3-16.
Couplers: Tightlock.   **Maximum Speed:** 100 m.p.h.
Seating Layout: 1: 2+2 facing, 2: 3+2 facing.
Dimensions: 20.89/20.06 x 2.80 m.
Braking: Disc, rheostatic & regenerative.
Multiple Working: Within class and with Classes 465 and 466.

DMCO(A). Lot No. 31133 1994–1995. 12/56. 46.7 t.
TSO. Lot No. 31134 1994–1995. –/59 1TD. 32.9 t.
PTSO. Lot No. 31135 1994–1995. –/68 1T. 34.6 t.
DMCO(B). Lot No. 31136 1994–1995. 12/56. 46.7 t.

365 501	CB	H	*SE*	RM	65894	72241	72240	65935
365 502	CB	H	*SE*	RM	65895	72243	72242	65936
365 503	CB	H	*SE*	RM	65896	72245	72244	65937
365 504	CB	H	*SE*	RM	65897	72247	72246	65938
365 505	CB	H	*SE*	RM	65898	72249	72248	65939
365 506	CB	H	*SE*	RM	65899	72251	72250	65940
365 507	CB	H	*SE*	RM	65900	72253	72252	65941
365 508	CB	H	*SE*	RM	65901	72255	72254	65942
365 509	CB	H	*SE*	RM	65902	72257	72256	65943
365 510	CB	H	*SE*	RM	65903	72259	72258	65944
365 511	CB	H	*SE*	RM	65904	72261	72260	65945
365 512	CB	H	*SE*	RM	65905	72263	72262	65946
365 513	CB	H	*SE*	RM	65906	72265	72264	65947
365 514	CB	H	*SE*	RM	65907	72267	72266	65948
365 515	CB	H	*SE*	RM	65908	72269	72268	65949
365 516	CB	H	*SE*	RM	65909	72271	72270	65950
365 517	NT	H	*WN*	HE	65910	72273	72272	65951
365 518	NT	H	*WN*	HE	65911	72275	72274	65952
365 519	NT	H	*WN*	HE	65912	72277	72276	65953

365 520	**NT**	H	*WN*	HE	65913	72279	72278	65954
365 521	**NT**	H	*WN*	HE	65914	72281	72280	65955
365 522	**NT**	H	*WN*	HE	65915	72283	72282	65956
365 523	**NT**	H	*WN*	HE	65916	72285	72284	65957
365 524	**NT**	H	*WN*	HE	65917	72287	72286	65958
365 525	**NT**	H	*WN*	HE	65918	72289	72288	65959
365 526	**NT**	H		ZC	65919	72291	72290	65960
365 527	**NT**	H	*WN*	HE	65920	72293	72292	65961
365 528	**NT**	H	*WN*	HE	65921	72295	72294	65962
365 529	**NT**	H	*WN*	HE	65922	72297	72296	65963
365 530	**NT**	H	*WN*	HE	65923	72299	72298	65964
365 531	**NT**	H	*WN*	HE	65924	72301	72300	65965
365 532	**NT**	H	*WN*	HE	65925	72303	72302	65966
365 533	**NT**	H	*WN*	HE	65926	72305	72304	65967
365 534	**NT**	H	*WN*	HE	65927	72307	72306	65968
365 535	**NT**	H	*WN*	HE	65928	72309	72308	65969
365 536	**NT**	H	*WN*	HE	65929	72311	72310	65970
365 537	**NT**	H	*WN*	HE	65930	72313	72312	65971
365 538	**NT**	H	*WN*	HE	65931	72315	72314	65972
365 539	**NT**	H	*WN*	HE	65932	72317	72316	65973
365 540	**NT**	H	*WN*	HE	65933	72319	72318	65974
365 541	**NT**	H	*WN*	HE	65934	72321	72320	65975

Names (Carried on one side of each DMCO):

365 505   Spirit of Ramsgate |365 515   Spirit of Dover

CLASS 375   ELECTROSTAR
ADTRANZ/BOMBARDIER DERBY

New South Eastern Trains (formerly Connex) units.
Systems: 25 kV AC overhead/750 V DC third rail (some third rail only with provision for retro-fitting of AC equipment).
Formations: Various.
Construction: Welded aluminium alloy underframe, sides and roof with steel ends. All sections bolted together.
Traction Motors: Two Adtranz 250 kW. **Doors:** Sliding plug.
Gangways: Throughout. **Bogies:** Adtranz P3-25/T3-25.
Couplers: Tightlock. **Maximum Speed:** 100 m.p.h.
Seating Layout: 2+2 facing/unidirectional (express units), 3+2 facing/unidirectional (outer suburban units). One coach per unit (or pair of units) normally "masquerades" as first class accommodation, but as these are effectively just standard class seats with antimacassars, they are included here as standard class.
Dimensions: 20.40/19.99 x 2.80 m.
Braking: Disc & regenerative. **Multiple Working:** Within class.

Class 375/3. Express units. 750 V DC only. DMSO(A)–TSO–DMSO(B).

DMSO(A). Bombardier Derby 2001–2002. –/60. 43.8 t.
TSO. Bombardier Derby 2001–2002. –/56 1TD 2W. 34.1 t.
DMSO(B). Bombardier Derby 2001–2002. –/60. 43.8 t.

375 301	**CN**	H	*SE*	RM	67921	74351	67931
375 302	**CN**	H	*SE*	RM	67922	74352	67932
375 303	**CN**	H	*SE*	RM	67923	74353	67933
375 304	**CN**	H	*SE*	RM	67924	74354	67934
375 305	**CN**	H	*SE*	RM	67925	74355	67935
375 306	**CN**	H	*SE*	RM	67926	74356	67936
375 307	**CN**	H	*SE*	RM	67927	74357	67937
375 308	**CN**	H	*SE*	RM	67928	74358	67938
375 309	**CN**	H	*SE*	RM	67929	74359	67939
375 310	**CN**	H	*SE*	RM	67930	74360	67940

Class 375/6. Express units. 25 kV AC/750 V DC DMSO(A)–MSO–PTSO–DMSO(B).

DMSO(A). Adtranz Derby 1999–2001. –/60. 43.8 t.
MSO. Adtranz Derby 1999–2001. –/66 1T. 40.5 t.
PTSO. Adtranz Derby 1999–2001. –/56 1TD 2W. 34.1 t.
DMSO(B). Adtranz Derby 1999–2001. –/60. 43.8 t.

Non-Standard livery: 375 610 is as **CN** but with blue doors instead of yellow and a gold band instead of a grey band on the lower bodyside (a special "Golden Jubilee" livery).

375 601	**CN**	H	*SE*	RM	67801	74251	74201	67851
375 602	**CN**	H	*SE*	RM	67802	74252	74202	67852
375 603	**CN**	H	*SE*	RM	67803	74253	74203	67853
375 604	**CN**	H	*SE*	RM	67804	74254	74204	67854
375 605	**CN**	H	*SE*	RM	67805	74255	74205	67855
375 606	**CN**	H	*SE*	RM	67806	74256	74206	67856
375 607	**CN**	H	*SE*	RM	67807	74257	74207	67857
375 608	**CN**	H	*SE*	RM	67808	74258	74208	67858
375 609	**CN**	H	*SE*	RM	67809	74259	74209	67859
375 610	**0**	H	*SE*	RM	67810	74260	74210	67860
375 611	**CN**	H	*SE*	RM	67811	74261	74211	67861
375 612	**CN**	H	*SE*	RM	67812	74262	74212	67862
375 613	**CN**	H	*SE*	RM	67813	74263	74213	67863
375 614	**CN**	H	*SE*	RM	67814	74264	74214	67864
375 615	**CN**	H	*SE*	RM	67815	74265	74215	67865
375 616	**CN**	H	*SE*	RM	67816	74266	74216	67866
375 617	**CN**	H	*SE*	RM	67817	74267	74217	67867
375 618	**CN**	H	*SE*	RM	67818	74268	74218	67868
375 619	**CN**	H	*SE*	RM	67819	74269	74219	67869
375 620	**CN**	H	*SE*	RM	67820	74270	74220	67870
375 621	**CN**	H	*SE*	RM	67821	74271	74221	67871
375 622	**CN**	H	*SE*	RM	67822	74272	74222	67872
375 623	**CN**	H	*SE*	RM	67823	74273	74223	67873
375 624	**CN**	H	*SE*	RM	67824	74274	74224	67874
375 625	**CN**	H	*SE*	RM	67825	74275	74225	67875
375 626	**CN**	H	*SE*	RM	67826	74276	74226	67876
375 627	**CN**	H	*SE*	RM	67827	74277	74227	67877
375 628	**CN**	H	*SE*	RM	67828	74278	74228	67878
375 629	**CN**	H	*SE*	RM	67829	74279	74229	67879
375 630	**CN**	H	*SE*	RM	67830	74280	74230	67880

Names (carried on one side of each DMSO):

375 608	BROMLEY TRAVELWISE		375 610	Royal Tunbridge Wells
375 611	Dr William Harvey		375 619	DRIVER JOHN NEVE
375 623	HOSPICE IN THE WEALD		375 624	White Cliffs Country

Class 375/7. Express units. 750 V DC only. DMSO(A)–MSO–TSO–DMSO(B).

DMSO(A). Bombardier Derby 2001–2002. –/60. 43.8 t.
MSO. Bombardier Derby 2001–2002. –/66 1T. 40.5 t.
TSO. Bombardier Derby 2001–2002. –/56 1TD 2W. 34.1 t.
DMSO(B). Bombardier Derby 2001–2002. –/60. 43.8 t.

375 701	**CN**	H	*SE*	RM	67831	74281	74231	67881
375 702	**CN**	H	*SE*	RM	67832	74282	74232	67882
375 703	**CN**	H	*SE*	RM	67833	74283	74233	67883
375 704	**CN**	H	*SE*	RM	67834	74284	74234	67884
375 705	**CN**	H	*SE*	RM	67835	74285	74235	67885
375 706	**CN**	H	*SE*	RM	67836	74286	74236	67886
375 707	**CN**	H	*SE*	RM	67837	74287	74237	67887
375 708	**CN**	H	*SE*	RM	67838	74288	74238	67888
375 709	**CN**	H	*SE*	RM	67839	74289	74239	67889
375 710	**CN**	H	*SE*	RM	67840	74290	74240	67890
375 711	**CN**	H	*SE*	RM	67841	74291	74241	67891
375 712	**CN**	H	*SE*	RM	67842	74292	74242	67892
375 713	**CN**	H	*SE*	RM	67843	74293	74243	67893
375 714	**CN**	H	*SE*	RM	67844	74294	74244	67894
375 715	**CN**	H	*SE*	RM	67845	74295	74245	67895

Name (carried on one side of each DMSO):

375 703   DICKENS TRAVELLER

Class 375/8. Express units. 750 V DC only. DMSO(A)–MSO–TSO–DMSO(B).
Similar to Class 375/7 but with modified shoegear. On order.

DMSO(A). Bombardier Derby 2004. –/ .   . t.
MSO. Bombardier Derby 2004. –/   1T.   . t.
TSO. Bombardier Derby 2004. –/   1TD 2W.   . t.
DMSO(B). Bombardier Derby 2004. –/ .   . t.

375 801	H	73301	79001	78201	73701
375 802	H	73302	79002	78202	73702
375 803	H	73303	79003	78203	73703
375 804	H	73304	79004	78204	73704
375 805	H	73305	79005	78205	73705
375 806	H	73306	79006	78206	73706
375 807	H	73307	79007	78207	73707
375 808	H	73308	79008	78208	73708
375 809	H	73309	79009	78209	73709
375 810	H	73310	79010	78210	73710
375 811	H	73311	79011	78211	73711
375 812	H	73312	79012	78212	73712
375 813	H	73313	79013	78213	73713
375 814	H	73314	79014	78214	73714

375 815	H	73315	79015	78215	73715
375 816	H	73316	79016	78216	73716
375 817	H	73317	79017	78217	73717
375 818	H	73318	79018	78218	73718
375 819	H	73319	79019	78219	73719
375 820	H	73320	79020	78220	73720
375 821	H	73321	79021	78221	73721
375 822	H	73322	79022	78222	73722
375 823	H	73323	79023	78223	73723
375 824	H	73324	79024	78224	73724
375 825	H	73325	79025	78225	73725
375 826	H	73326	79026	78226	73726
375 827	H	73327	79027	78227	73727
375 828	H	73328	/9028	70228	73728
375 829	H	73329	79029	78229	73729
375 830	H	73330	79030	78230	73730

Class 375/9. Outer suburban units. 750 V DC only. DMSO(A)–MSO–TSO–DMSO(B).

DMSO(A). Bombardier Derby 2003–2004. –/71. 43.4 t.
MSO. Bombardier Derby 2003–2004. –/73 1T. 39.3 t.
TSO. Bombardier Derby 2003–2004. –/59 1TD 2W. 35.6 t.
DMSO(B). Bombardier Derby 2003–2004. –/71. 43.4 t.

375 901	CN	H	73331	79031	79061	73731
375 902	CN	H	73332	79032	79062	73732
375 903	CN	H	73333	79033	79063	73733
375 904	CN	H	73334	79034	79064	73734
375 905	CN	H	73335	79035	79065	73735
375 906	CN	H	73336	79036	79066	73736
375 907	CN	H	73337	79037	79067	73737
375 908	CN	H	73338	79038	79068	73738
375 909	CN	H	73339	79039	79069	73739
375 910	CN	H	73340	79040	79070	73740
375 911	CN	H	73341	79041	79071	73741
375 912	CN	H	73342	79042	79072	73742
375 913	CN	H	73343	79043	79073	73743
375 914	CN	H	73344	79044	79074	73744
375 915	CN	H	73345	79045	79075	73745
375 916	CN	H	73346	79046	79076	73746
375 917	CN	H	73347	79047	79077	73747
375 918	CN	H	73348	79048	79078	73748
375 919	CN	H	73349	79049	79079	73749
375 920	CN	H	73350	79050	79080	73750
375 921	CN	H	73351	79051	79081	73751
375 922	CN	H	73352	79052	79082	73752
375 923	CN	H	73353	79053	79083	73753
375 924	CN	H	73354	79054	79084	73754
375 925	CN	H	73355	79055	79085	73755
375 926	CN	H	73356	79056	79086	73756
375 927	CN	H	73357	79057	79087	73757

CLASS 376 ELECTROSTAR BOMBARDIER DERBY

New units on order for South Eastern Trains. For inner suburban services. Full details awaited.
Systems: 750 V DC third rail.
Formations: DMSO(A)–MSO–TSO–MSO–DMSO(B).
Seating layout: 2+2.

376 001	61101	63301	64301	63501	61601
376 002	61102	63302	64302	63502	61602
376 003	61103	63303	64303	63503	61603
376 004	61104	63304	64304	63504	61604
376 005	61105	63305	64305	63505	61605
376 006	61106	63306	64306	63506	61606
376 007	61107	63307	64307	63507	61607
376 008	61108	63308	64308	63508	61608
376 009	61109	63309	64309	63509	61609
376 010	61110	63310	64310	63510	61610
376 011	61111	63311	64311	63511	61611
376 012	61112	63312	64312	63512	61612
376 013	61113	63313	64313	63513	61613
376 014	61114	63314	64314	63514	61614
376 015	61115	63315	64315	63515	61615
376 016	61116	63316	64316	63516	61616
376 017	61117	63317	64317	63517	61617
376 018	61118	63318	64318	63518	61618
376 019	61119	63319	64319	63519	61619
376 020	61120	63320	64320	63520	61620
376 021	61121	63321	64321	63521	61621
376 022	61122	63322	64322	63522	61622
376 023	61123	63323	64323	63523	61623
376 024	61124	63324	64324	63524	61624
376 025	61125	63325	64325	63525	61625
376 026	61126	63326	64326	63526	61626
376 027	61127	63327	64327	63527	61627
376 028	61128	63328	64328	63528	61628
376 029	61129	63329	64329	63529	61629
376 030	61130	63330	64330	63530	61630
376 031	61131	63331	64331	63531	61631
376 032	61132	63332	64332	63532	61632
376 033	61133	63333	64333	63533	61633
376 034	61134	63334	64334	63534	61634
376 035	61135	63335	64335	63535	61635
376 036	61136	63336	64336	63536	61636

CLASS 377 ELECTROSTAR BOMBARDIER DERBY

New South Central units.
Systems: 25 kV AC overhead/750 V DC third rail or third rail only with provision for retro-fitting of AC equipment.
Formations: Various.
Construction: Welded aluminium alloy underframe, sides and roof with steel ends. All sections bolted together.

Traction Motors: Two Bombardier 250 kW.	**Doors**: Sliding plug.
Gangways: Throughout.	**Bogies**: Bombardier P3-25/T3-25.
Couplers: Dellner 12.	**Maximum Speed**: 100 m.p.h.
Seating Layout: Various.	**Dimensions**: 20.40/19.99 x 2.80 m.
Braking: Disc & regenerative.	**Multiple Working**: Within class.

Class 377/1. 750 V DC only. DMSO(A)–MSO–TSO–DMSO(B).
Seating layout: 2+2 (377 101–377 119), 3+2 and 2+2 (377 120–377 164). Some seats "masquerade" as first class accommodation, but as these are effectively just standard class seats with antimacassars, they are included here as standard class.

DMSO(A). Bombardier Derby 2002–2003. –/60 (s –/68, t –/60). 43.4 t.
MSO. Bombardier Derby 2002–2003. –/66 (s –/70, t –/70). 1T. 39.0 t.
TSO. Bombardier Derby 2002–2003. –/56 (s –/60, t –/54). 1TD 2W. 35.4 t.
DMSO(B). Bombardier Derby 2002–2003. –/60 (s –/68, t –/60). 43.4 t.

377 101		**SN**	P	*SC*	BI	78501	77101	78901	78701
377 102		**SN**	P	*SC*	BI	78502	77102	78902	78702
377 103		**SN**	P	*SC*	BI	78503	77103	78903	78703
377 104		**SN**	P	*SC*	BI	78504	77104	78904	78704
377 105		**SN**	P	*SC*	BI	78505	77105	78905	78705
377 106		**SN**	P	*SC*	BI	78506	77106	78906	78706
377 107		**SN**	P	*SC*	BI	78507	77107	78907	78707
377 108		**SN**	P	*SC*	BI	78508	77108	78908	78708
377 109		**SN**	P	*SC*	BI	78509	77109	78909	78709
377 110		**SN**	P	*SC*	BI	78510	77110	78910	78710
377 111		**SN**	P	*SC*	BI	78511	77111	78911	78711
377 112		**SN**	P	*SC*	BI	78512	77112	78912	78712
377 113		**SN**	P	*SC*	BI	78513	77113	78913	78713
377 114		**SN**	P	*SC*	BI	78514	77114	78914	78714
377 115		**SN**	P	*SC*	BI	78515	77115	78915	78715
377 116		**SN**	P	*SC*	BI	78516	77116	78916	78716
377 117		**SN**	P	*SC*	BI	78517	77117	78917	78717
377 118		**SN**	P	*SC*	BI	78518	77118	78918	78718
377 119		**SN**	P	*SC*	BI	78519	77119	78919	78719
377 120	s	**SN**	P	*SC*	BI	78520	77120	78920	78720
377 121	s	**SN**	P	*SC*	BI	78521	77121	78921	78721
377 122	s	**SN**	P	*SC*	BI	78522	77122	78922	78722
377 123	s	**SN**	P	*SC*	BI	78523	77123	78923	78723
377 124	s	**SN**	P	*SC*	BI	78524	77124	78924	78724
377 125	s	**SN**	P	*SC*	BI	78525	77125	78925	78725
377 126	s	**SN**	P	*SC*	BI	78526	77126	78926	78726

377 127	s	**SN**	P	*SC*	BI	78527	77127	78927	78727
377 128	s	**SN**	P	*SC*	BI	78528	77128	78928	78728
377 129	s	**SN**	P	*SC*	BI	78529	77129	78929	78729
377 130	s	**SN**	P	*SC*	BI	78530	77130	78930	78730
377 131	s	**SN**	P	*SC*	BI	78531	77131	78931	78731
377 132	s	**SN**	P	*SC*	BI	78532	77132	78932	78732
377 133	s	**SN**	P	*SC*	BI	78533	77133	78933	78733
377 134	s	**SN**	P	*SC*	BI	78534	77134	78934	78734
377 135	s	**SN**	P	*SC*	BI	78535	77135	78935	78735
377 136	s	**SN**	P	*SC*	BI	78536	77136	78936	78736
377 137	s	**SN**	P	*SC*	BI	78537	77137	78937	78737
377 138	s	**SN**	P	*SC*	BI	78538	77138	78938	78738
377 139	s	**SN**	P	*SC*	BI	78539	77139	78939	78739
377 140	t	**SN**	P	*SC*	BI	78540	77140	78940	78740
377 141	t	**SN**	P	*SC*	BI	78541	77141	78941	78741
377 142	t	**SN**	P	*SC*	BI	78542	77142	78942	78742
377 143	t	**SN**	P	*SC*	BI	78543	77143	78943	78743
377 144	t	**SN**	P	*SC*	BI	78544	77144	78944	78744
377 145	t	**SN**	P	*SC*	BI	78545	77145	78945	78745
377 146	t	**SN**	P	*SC*	BI	78546	77146	78946	78746
377 147	t	**SN**	P	*SC*	BI	78547	77147	78947	78747
377 148	t	**SN**	P	*SC*	BI	78548	77148	78948	78748
377 149	t	**SN**	P	*SC*	BI	78549	77149	78949	78749
377 150	t	**SN**	P	*SC*	BI	78550	77150	78950	78750
377 151	t	**SN**	P	*SC*	BI	78551	77151	78951	78751
377 152	t	**SN**	P	*SC*	BI	78552	77152	78952	78752
377 153	t	**SN**	P	*SC*	BI	78553	77153	78953	78753
377 154	t	**SN**	P	*SC*	BI	78554	77154	78954	78754
377 155	t	**SN**	P	*SC*	BI	78555	77155	78955	78755
377 156	t	**SN**	P	*SC*	BI	78556	77156	78956	78756
377 157	t	**SN**	P	*SC*	BI	78557	77157	78957	78757
377 158	t	**SN**	P	*SC*	BI	78558	77158	78958	78758
377 159	t	**SN**	P	*SC*	BI	78559	77159	78959	78759
377 160	t	**SN**	P	*SC*	BI	78560	77160	78960	78760
377 161	t	**SN**	P	*SC*	BI	78561	77161	78961	78761
377 162	t	**SN**	P	*SC*	BI	78562	77162	78962	78762
377 163	t	**SN**	P	*SC*	BI	78563	77163	78963	78763
377 164	t	**SN**	P	*SC*	BI	78564	77164	78964	78764

Class 377/2. 25 kV AC/750 V DC. DMSO(A)–MSO–PTSO–DMSO(B). Details awaited.

DMSO(A). Bombardier Derby 2003–2004. –/ . 43.8 t.
MSO. Bombardier Derby 2003–2004. –/ 1T. 40.5 t.
PTSO. Bombardier Derby 2003–2004. –/ 1TD 2W. 34.1 t.
DMSO(B). Bombardier Derby 2003–2004. –/ . 43.8 t.

377 201	**SN**	P		78571	77171	78971	78771
377 202	**SN**	P		78572	77172	78972	78772
377 203	**SN**	P		78573	77173	78973	78773
377 204	**SN**	P		78574	77174	78974	78774
377 205	**SN**	P		78575	77175	78975	78775

377 206	**SN**	P			78576	77176	78976	78776
377 207	**SN**	P			78577	77177	78977	78777
377 208	**SN**	P			78578	77178	78978	78778
377 209	**SN**	P			78579	77179	78979	78779
377 210	**SN**	P			78580	77180	78980	78780
377 211	**SN**	P			78581	77181	78981	78781
377 212	**SN**	P			78582	77182	78982	78782
377 213	**SN**	P			78583	77183	78983	78783
377 214	**SN**	P			78584	77184	78984	78784
377 215	**SN**	P			78585	77185	78985	78785

Class 377/3. 750 V DC only. DMSO(A)–TSO–DMSO(B).

Units built as Class 376, to be renumbered in the Class 377/3 range when the couplers are changed from Tightlock to Dellner.
Seating Layout: 2+2 facing/undirectional.

DMSO(A). Bombardier Derby 2001–2002. –/60. 45.3 t.
TSO. Bombardier Derby 2001–2002. –/56 1TD 2W. 40.2 t.
DMSO(B). Bombardier Derby 2001–2002. –/60. 45.3 t.

377 301	(375 311)	**SN**	P	*SC*	BI	68201	74801	68401
377 302	(375 312)	**SN**	P	*SC*	BI	68202	74802	68402
377 303	(375 313)	**SN**	P	*SC*	BI	68203	74803	68403
377 304	(375 314)	**SN**	P	*SC*	BI	68204	74804	68404
377 305	(375 315)	**SN**	P	*SC*	BI	68205	74805	68405
377 306	(375 316)	**SN**	P	*SC*	BI	68206	74806	68406
377 307	(375 317)	**SN**	P	*SC*	BI	68207	74807	68407
377 308	(375 318)	**SN**	P	*SC*	BI	68208	74808	68408
377 309	(375 319)	**SN**	P	*SC*	BI	68209	74809	68409
377 310	(375 320)	**SN**	P	*SC*	BI	68210	74810	68410
377 311	(375 321)	**SN**	P	*SC*	BI	68211	74811	68411
377 312	(375 322)	**SN**	P	*SC*	BI	68212	74812	68412
377 313	(375 323)	**SN**	P	*SC*	BI	68213	74813	68413
377 314	(375 324)	**SN**	P	*SC*	BI	68214	74814	68414
377 315	(375 325)	**SN**	P	*SC*	BI	68215	74815	68415
377 316	(375 326)	**SN**	P	*SC*	BI	68216	74816	68416
377 317	(375 327)	**SN**	P	*SC*	BI	68217	74817	68417
377 318	(375 328)	**SN**	P	*SC*	BI	68218	74818	68418
377 319	(375 329)	**SN**	P	*SC*	BI	68219	74819	68419
377 320	(375 330)	**SN**	P	*SC*	BI	68220	74820	68420
377 321	(375 331)	**SN**	P	*SC*	BI	68221	74821	68421
377 322	(375 332)	**SN**	P	*SC*	BI	68222	74822	68422
377 323	(375 333)	**SN**	P	*SC*	BI	68223	74823	68423
377 324	(375 334)	**SN**	P	*SC*	BI	68224	74824	68424
377 325	(375 335)	**SN**	P	*SC*	BI	68225	74825	68425
377 326	(375 336)	**SN**	P	*SC*	BI	68226	74826	68426
377 327	(375 337)	**SN**	P	*SC*	BI	68227	74827	68427
377 328	(375 338)	**SN**	P	*SC*	BI	68228	74828	68428

Class 377/4. Details awaited. DMSO–MSO–TSO–DMSO. On order.

377 401	**SN**	P		73401	78801	78601	73801
377 402	**SN**	P		73402	78802	78602	73802
377 403	**SN**	P		73403	78803	78603	73803
377 404	**SN**	P		73404	78804	78604	73804
377 405	**SN**	P		73405	78805	78605	73805
377 406	**SN**	P		73406	78806	78606	73806
377 407	**SN**	P		73407	78807	78607	73807
377 408	**SN**	P		73408	78808	78608	73808
377 409	**SN**	P		73409	78809	78609	73809
377 410	**SN**	P		73410	78810	78610	73810
377 411	**SN**	P		73411	78811	78611	73811
377 412	**SN**	P		73412	78812	78612	73812
377 413	**SN**	P		73413	78813	78613	73813
377 414	**SN**	P		73414	78814	78614	73814
377 415	**SN**	P		73415	78815	78615	73815
377 416	**SN**	P		73416	78816	78616	73816
377 417	**SN**	P		73417	78817	78617	73817
377 418	**SN**	P		73418	78818	78618	73818
377 419	**SN**	P		73419	78819	78619	73819
377 420	**SN**	P		73420	78820	78620	73820
377 421	**SN**	P		73421	78821	78621	73821
377 422	**SN**	P		73422	78822	78622	73822
377 423	**SN**	P		73423	78823	78623	73823
377 424	**SN**	P		73424	78824	78624	73824
377 425	**SN**	P		73425	78825	78625	73825
377 426	**SN**	P		73426	78826	78626	73826
377 427	**SN**	P		73427	78827	78627	73827
377 428	**SN**	P		73428	78828	78628	73828
377 429	**SN**	P		73429	78829	78629	73829
377 430	**SN**	P		73430	78830	78630	73830
377 431	**SN**	P		73431	78831	78631	73831
377 432	**SN**	P		73432	78832	78632	73832
377 433	**SN**	P		73433	78833	78633	73833
377 434	**SN**	P		73434	78834	78634	73834
377 435	**SN**	P		73435	78835	78635	73835
377 436	**SN**	P		73436	78836	78636	73836
377 437	**SN**	P		73437	78837	78637	73837
377 438	**SN**	P		73438	78838	78638	73838
377 439	**SN**	P		73439	78839	78639	73839
377 440	**SN**	P		73440	78840	78640	73840
377 441	**SN**	P		73441	78841	78641	73841
377 442	**SN**	P		73442	78842	78642	73842
377 443	**SN**	P		73443	78843	78643	73843
377 444	**SN**	P		73444	78844	78644	73844
377 445	**SN**	P		73445	78845	78645	73845
377 446	**SN**	P		73446	78846	78646	73846
377 447	**SN**	P		73447	78847	78647	73847
377 448	**SN**	P		73448	78848	78648	73848
377 449	**SN**	P		73449	78849	78649	73849

377 450	**SN**	P	73450	78850	78650	73850
377 451	**SN**	P	73451	78851	78651	73851
377 452	**SN**	P	73452	78852	78652	73852
377 453	**SN**	P	73453	78853	78653	73853
377 454	**SN**	P	73454	78854	78654	73854
377 455	**SN**	P	73455	78855	78655	73855
377 456	**SN**	P	73456	78856	78656	73856
377 457	**SN**	P	73457	78857	78657	73857
377 458	**SN**	P	73458	78858	78658	73858
377 459	**SN**	P	73459	78859	78659	73859
377 460	**SN**	P	73460	78860	78660	73860
377 461	**SN**	P	73461	78861	78661	73861
377 462	**SN**	P	73462	78862	78662	73862
377 463	**SN**	P	73463	78863	78663	73863
377 464	**SN**	P	73464	78864	78664	73864
377 465	**SN**	P	73465	78865	78665	73865
377 466	**SN**	P	73466	78866	78666	73866
377 467	**SN**	P	73467	78867	78667	73867
377 468	**SN**	P	73468	78868	78668	73868
377 469	**SN**	P	73469	78869	78669	73869
377 470	**SN**	P	73470	78870	78670	73870
377 471	**SN**	P	73471	78871	78671	73871
377 472	**SN**	P	73472	78872	78672	73872
377 473	**SN**	P	73473	78873	78673	73873
377 474	**SN**	P	73474	78874	78674	73874
377 475	**SN**	P	73475	78875	78675	73875

CLASS 390 PENDOLINO ALSTOM BIRMINGHAM

New tilting units for Virgin West Coast.
Formation: DMRFO–MFO–PTFO–MFO–(TSO)–MSO–PTSRMB–MSO–DMSO.
Construction: Welded aluminium alloy.
Traction Motors: Two Alstom ONIX 800 of 425 kW.
Doors: Sliding plug.
Gangways: Within unit.   **Bogies:** Fiat-SIG.
Couplers: Dellner.   **Maximum Speed:** 140 m.p.h.
Seating Layout: 1: 2+1 facing 2: 2+2 facing/unidirectional.
Dimensions: 23.05 (outer) 23.90 (inner) x 2.73 m.
Braking: Disc, rheostatic & regenerative.
Multiple Working: Within class.

DMKFO: Alstom Birmingham 2001–2004. 18/–. 55.6 t.
MFOD: Alstom Birmingham 2001–2004. 39/– 1TD 1W. 52.0 t.
PTFO: Alstom Birmingham 2001–2004. 44/– 1T. 50.1 t.
MFO: Alstom Birmingham 2001–2004. 46/– 1T. 51.8 t.
TSO: Alstom Birmingham 2001–2004. –/76 1T. 45.5 t.
MSO(A): Alstom Birmingham 2001–2004. –/66 1TD 1W. 50.0 t.
PTSRMB: Alstom Birmingham 2001–2004. –/48. 52.0 t.
MSO(B): Alstom Birmingham 2001–2004. –/64 1TD 1W. 51.7 t.
DMSO: Alstom Birmingham 2001–2004. –/46 1T. 51.0 t.

Note: These units have so far been delivered as 8-car sets, without the TSO (688xx). Units from 390 035 are to be delivered as 9-car units and other units will be retro-fitted during 2004.

390 001	**VT**	A			69101	69401	69501	69601	68801
					69701	69801	69901	69201	
390 002	**VT**	A			69102	69402	69502	69602	68802
					69702	69802	69902	69202	
390 003	**VT**	A	*VW*	MA	69103	69403	69503	69603	68803
					69703	69803	69903	69203	
390 004	**VT**	A	*VW*	MA	69104	69404	69504	69604	68804
					69704	69804	69904	69204	
390 005	**VT**	A	*VW*	MA	69105	69405	69505	69605	68805
					69705	69805	69905	69205	
390 006	**VT**	A	*VW*	MA	69106	69406	69506	69606	68806
					69706	69806	69906	69206	
390 007	**VT**	A	*VW*	MA	69107	69407	69507	69607	68807
					69707	69807	69907	69207	
390 008	**VT**	A			69108	69408	69508	69608	68808
					69708	69808	69908	69208	
390 009	**VT**	A	*VW*	MA	69109	69409	69509	69609	68809
					69709	69809	69909	69209	
390 010	**VT**	A	*VW*	MA	69110	69410	69510	69610	68810
					69710	69810	69910	69210	
390 011	**VT**	A	*VW*	MA	69111	69411	69511	69611	68811
					69711	69811	69911	69211	
390 012	**VT**	A	*VW*	MA	69112	69412	69512	69612	68812
					69712	69812	69912	69212	
390 013	**VT**	A	*VW*	MA	69113	69413	69513	69613	68813
					69713	69813	69913	69213	
390 014	**VT**	A	*VW*	MA	69114	69414	69514	69614	68814
					69714	69814	69914	69214	
390 015	**VT**	A	*VW*	MA	69115	69415	69515	69615	68815
					69715	69815	69915	69215	
390 016	**VT**	A	*VW*	MA	69116	69416	69516	69616	68816
					69716	69816	69916	69216	
390 017	**VT**	A	*VW*	MA	69117	69417	69517	69617	68817
					69717	69817	69917	69217	
390 018	**VT**	A	*VW*	MA	69118	69418	69518	69618	68818
					69718	69818	69918	69218	
390 019	**VT**	A	*VW*	MA	69119	69419	69519	69619	68819
					69719	69819	69919	69219	
390 020	**VT**	A	*VW*	MA	69120	69420	69520	69620	68820
					69720	69820	69920	69220	
390 021	**VT**	A	*VW*	MA	69121	69421	69521	69621	68821
					69721	69821	69921	69221	
390 022	**VT**	A	*VW*	MA	69122	69422	69522	69622	68822
					69722	69822	69922	69222	
390 023	**VT**	A	*VW*	MA	69123	69423	69523	69623	68823
					69723	69823	69923	69223	

390 024	**VT**	A	*VW*	MA	69124	69424	69524	69624	68824
					69724	69824	69924	69224	
390 025	**VT**	A	*VW*	MA	69125	69425	69525	69625	68825
					69725	69825	69925	69225	
390 026	**VT**	A	*VW*	MA	69126	69426	69526	69626	68826
					69726	69826	69926	69226	
390 027	**VT**	A	*VW*	MA	69127	69427	69527	69627	68827
					69727	69827	69927	69227	
390 028	**VT**	A	*VW*	MA	69128	69428	69528	69628	68828
					69728	69828	69928	69228	
390 029	**VT**	A	*VW*	MA	69129	69429	69529	69629	68829
					69729	69829	69929	69229	
390 030	**VT**	A	*VW*	MA	69130	69430	69530	69630	68830
					69730	69830	69930	69230	
390 031	**VT**	A	*VW*	MA	69131	69431	69531	69631	68831
					69731	69831	69931	69231	
390 032	**VT**	A	*VW*	MA	69132	69432	69532	69632	68832
					69732	69832	69932	69232	
390 033	**VT**	A			69133	69433	69533	69633	68833
					69733	69833	69933	69233	
390 034	**VT**	A			69134	69434	69534	69634	68834
					69734	69834	69934	69234	
390 035	**VT**	A			69135	69435	69535	69635	68835
					69735	69835	69935	69235	
390 036	**VT**	A			69136	69436	69536	69636	68836
					69736	69836	69936	69236	
390 037	**VT**	A			69137	69437	69537	69637	68837
					69737	69837	69937	69237	
390 038	**VT**	A			69138	69438	69538	69638	68838
					69738	69838	69938	69238	
390 039	**VT**	A			69139	69439	69539	69639	68839
					69739	69839	69939	69239	
390 040	**VT**	A			69140	69440	69540	69640	68840
					69740	69840	69940	69240	
390 041	**VT**	A			69141	69441	69541	69641	68841
					69741	69841	69941	69241	
390 042	**VT**	A			69142	69442	69542	69642	68842
					69742	69842	69942	69242	
390 043	**VT**	A			69143	69443	69543	69643	68843
					69743	69843	69943	69243	
390 044	**VT**	A			69144	69444	69544	69644	68844
					69744	69844	69944	69244	
390 045	**VT**	A			69145	69445	69545	69645	68845
					69745	69845	69945	69245	
390 046	**VT**	A			69146	69446	69546	69646	68846
					69746	69846	69946	69246	
390 047	**VT**	A			69147	69447	69547	69647	68847
					69747	69847	69947	69247	
390 048	**VT**	A			69148	69448	69548	69648	68848
					69748	69848	69948	69248	

390 049	**VT**	A	69149	69449	69549	69649	68849
			69749	69849	69949	69249	
390 050	**VT**	A	69150	69450	69550	69650	68850
			69750	69850	69950	69250	
390 051	**VT**	A	69151	69451	69551	69651	68851
			69751	69851	69951	69251	
390 052	**VT**	A	69152	69452	69552	69652	68852
			69752	69852	69952	69252	
390 053	**VT**	A	69153	69453	69553	69653	68853
			69753	69853	69953	69253	

Names (carried on MFO No. 696xx):

390 001	Virgin Pioneer	390 028	City of Preston
390 002	Virgin Angel	390 029	City of Stoke-on-Trent
390 003	Virgin Hero	390 030	City of Edinburgh
390 004	Virgin Scot	390 031	City of Liverpool
390 005	City of Wolverhampton	390 032	City of Birmingham
390 006	Mission Possible	390 033	City of Glasgow
390 007	Virgin Lady	390 034	City of Carlisle
390 008	Virgin King	390 035	City of Lancaster
390 009	Virgin Queen	390 036	City of Coventry
390 010	Commonwealth Games 2002	390 037	Virgin Difference
390 011	City of Lichfield	390 038	City of London
390 012	Virgin Star	390 039	Virgin Quest
390 013	Virgin Spirit	390 040	
390 014	City of Manchester	390 041	
390 015	Virgin Crusader	390 042	
390 016	Virgin Champion	390 043	
390 017	Virgin Prince	390 044	
390 018	Virgin Princess	390 045	
390 019	Virgin Warrior	390 046	
390 020	Virgin Cavalier	390 047	
390 021	Virgin Dream	390 048	
390 022	Virgin Hope	390 049	
390 023	Virgin Glory	390 050	
390 024	Virgin Venturer	390 051	
390 025	Virgin Stagecoach	390 052	
390 026	Virgin Enterprise	390 053	
390 027	Virgin Buccaneer		

2. 750 V DC THIRD RAIL EMUs

These classes use the third rail system at 750–850 V DC. Buffet cars have electric cooking. In addition to the class number, the old SR designations e.g. 4 Vep are quoted. Outer couplings are buckeyes on units built before 1982 with bar couplings within the units. Newer units have tightlock outer couplers. All units of Classes 411, 421 and 423 were due for withdrawal by the end of 2004, under the SRA's original plans for disposal of slam door rolling stock, although several are likely to be in service in 2005.

CLASS 411   BR EASTLEIGH

Units built for the Kent Coast Electrification. Refurbished and fitted with hopper ventilators, "Inter-City 70" seats and fluorescent lighting.

SR designation: 3 Cep or 4 Cep.
Formation: DMSO(A)–TBCK–TSO–DMSO(B).
Construction: Steel. **Doors:** Slam.
Gangways: Throughout. **Electrical Equipment:** 1966-type.
Traction Motors: Two EE507 of 185 kW. **Couplers:** Buckeye.
Bogies: One Mk. 4 (* Mark 3B, † Mark 6) motor bogie (DMSO). Commonwealth († B5 (SR)) trailer bogies.
Maximum Speed: 90 m.p.h. **Dimensions:** 20.18 x 2.82 m.
Seating Layout: 1: Compartments, 2: 2+2 facing (one compartment in TBCK).
Braking: Tread brakes.
Multiple Working: Within class and with Classes 412, 421, 422, 423, 438 and locos of Classes 33/1 and 73.

DMSO (A). –/64. 44.2 t.
TBCK. 24/6 2T. 36.2 t.
TSOL. –/64 2T. 33.8 t.
DMSO (B). –/64. 43.5 t.

Lot numbers are as follows, all cars being built at Eastleigh:

61229–61237. 30449 1958.		**70261–70268.** 30455 1958–1959.	
61307–61407. 30454 1958–1959.		**70304–70354.** 30456 1958–1959.	
61698–61808. 30619 1960–1961.		**70503–70550.** 30620 1960–1961.	
61950–61959. 30708 1963.		**70552–70609.** 30621 1960–1961.	
70229–70233. 30450 1958.		**70654–70657.** 30709 1963.	
70235–70239. 30451 1958.		**70664.** 30710 1963.	
70241. 30640 1961.			

71626–71636. Converted at Swindon 1981–1983 from loco-hauled TSO of various lots.
71711. Converted at Swindon 1981–1983 from loco-hauled TSO. Former numbers are as follows:

71626 (3916)	71629 (3992)	71636 (4065)
71627 (3921)	71632 (4063)	71711 (3994)

Class 411/9. South West Trains unit with TSO removed (DMSO–TBCK–DMSO) Unit generally dedicated to Brockenhurst to Lymington Harbour shuttles.

| 1199 | | **ST** | P | *SW* | FR | 61329 | 70578 | 61328 | |

Class 411/5. Standard units.

1512		**ST**	P		BM	61321		70268	61320
1517		**ST**	P	*SW*	FR	61317	70309	70266	61316
1519		**ST**	P	*SW*	FR	61403	70352	70536	61402
1527		**N**	P		BM	61237	70239	70233	61238
1531		**ST**	P	*SW*	FR	61233	70237	70231	61234
1533		**ST**	P	*SW*	FR	61393	70347	71627	61385
1534		**ST**	P	*SW*	FR	61405	70353	71626	61404
1535		**ST**	P	*SW*	FR	61397	70349	71629	61396
1539		**ST**	P	*SW*	FR	61401	70351	71632	61400
1544		**ST**	P	*SW*	FR	61315	70308	70265	61349
1550		**ST**	P	*SW*	FR	61313	70307	70264	61312
1553		**ST**	P	*SW*	FR	61728	70306	70263	61350
1555		**ST**	P	*SW*	FR	61311	70326	70283	61310
1562		**N**	P	*SE*	RM	61407	70236	70241	61406
1563	*	**ST**	P	*SW*	FR	61740	70575	70526	61741
1565	*	**ST**	P	*SW*	FR	61762	70311	71711	61763
1571	*	**ST**	P	*SW*	FF	61806	70608	70289	61807
1573	*	**ST**	P	*SW*	FR	61726	70568	70519	61727
1578	*	**ST**	P	*SW*	FR	61700	70555	70506	61701
1581	*	**ST**	P	*SW*	FR	61784	70597	70548	61785
1590	*	**N**	P	*SE*	RM	61696	70553	70504	61697
1592	*	**G**	P	*SE*	RM	61778	70594	70545	61779
1593	*	**N**	P	*SE*	RM	61730	70570	70521	61731
1594	*	**N**	P	*SE*	RM	61754	70582	70533	61755
1602	*	**CX**	P	*SE*	RM	61958	70565	70279	61959
1612	*	**ST**	P	*SW*	FR	61794	70602	70535	61795
1615	*	**N**	P	*SE*	RM	61956	70657	70664	61957
1697	†	**ST**	P	*SW*	FR	61373	70337	70294	61372
1698	†	**ST**	P	*SW*	FR	61355	70343	70300	61384
1699	†	**ST**	P	*SW*	FR	61712	70561	70512	61713
Spare	*	**N**	P		BM	61734			61735

CLASS 412   BR EASTLEIGH

All Reformed in 2002. For details see Class 411 above except **69341–69347**.
Class 412/1. "Greyhound" 4 Cep. These are former Beps which were reformed in 2002. They have had their buffet cars removed and replaced by TSOs.
Formation: DMSO(A)–TBCK–TSO–DMSO(B).

2311	(2301)	**ST**	P	*SW*	FR	61804	70607	70539	61805
2312	(2302)	**ST**	P	*SW*	FR	61774	70592	70295	61809
2313	(2303)	**ST**	P	*SW*	FR	61954	70656	71636	61955
2314	(2304)	**ST**	P	*SW*	FR	61736	70573	70517	61737
2315	(2305)	**ST**	P	*SW*	FR	61798	70354	70229	61799
2316	(2306)	**ST**	P	*SW*	FR	61808	70609	70272	61775
2317	(2307)	**ST**	P	*SW*	FR	61802	70606	70261	61803

Class 412/2. 4 Bep. These are former Ceps which were reformed in 2002. They have had their TSOs removed and replaced by buffet cars.
Formation: DMSO(A)–TBCK–TSRB–DMSO(B).

69341–69347. TSRB. Lot No. 30622 1961. Converted from TRB to TSRB at BREL Swindon 1982–84. –/24 1T + 9 longitudinal buffet chairs. 35.5 t.

2321	(1568)	†	**ST**	P	*SW*	FR	61766	70588	69341	61767
2322	(1548)	†	**ST**	P	*SW*	FR	61375	70338	69342	61374
2324	(1566)	†	**ST**	P	*SW*	FR	61722	70566	69344	61723
2325	(1537)	†	**ST**	P	*SW*	FR	61229	70235	69345	61230
2327	(1538)	†	**ST**	P	*SW*	FR	61307	70304	69347	61306

Former numbers of converted buffet cars:

| 69341 (69014) | 69344 (69012) | 69347 (69015) |
| 69342 (69019) | 69345 (69013) | |

CLASS 421   BR YORK

Units built for Portsmouth and Brighton lines. Facelifted with new trim and fluorescent lighting in saloons.

SR designation: 4 Cig.
Formation: DTCso(A)–MBSO–TSO–DTCso(B).
Construction: Steel.   **Doors:** Slam.
Gangways: Throughout.   **Electrical Equipment:** 1966-type.
Traction Motors: Four EE507 of 185 kW. **Couplers:** Buckeye.
Bogies: Two Mk. 4 or Mk. 6 motor bogies (MBSO). B5 (SR) bogies (trailer cars).
Maximum Speed: 90 m.p.h.   **Dimensions:** 20.18 x 2.82 m.
Seating Layout: 1: Compartments, 2: 2+2 facing (plus one four-a-side compartment per DTC).
Braking: Tread brakes.
Multiple Working: Within class and with Classes 411, 412, 423, 438 and locos of Classes 33/1 and 73.

Phase 1 sets. These have SR Mark 4 motor bogies.

76076–76129. DTCsoL(A). Lot No. 30741 1964–1965. 18/36 2T (–/54 2T†, –/60 2T§). 35.5 t.
62017–62070.MBSO. Lot No. 30742 1964–1965. –/56. 49 t.
70695–70730. TSO. Lot No. 30730 1964–1965. –/72. 31.5 t.
71044–71097. TSO. Lot No. 30817 1970. –/72. 31.5 t.
71766–71770. TSO. Lot No. 30784 1964–1965. –/72. 31.5 t.
76022–76075. DTCsoL(B). Lot No. 30740 1964–1965. 24/28 2T.

Phase 2 sets. These have SR Mark 6 motor bogies.

76561–76570. DTCso(A). Lot No. 30802 1970. 18/36 2T (–/54 2T†, –/60 2T§). 35.5 t.
76581–76610. DTCso(A). Lot No. 30806 1970. 18/36 2T (–/54 2T†, –/60 2T§). 35.5 t.
76717–76787. DTCso(A). Lot No. 30814 1970–1972. 18/36 2T (–/54 2T†, –/60 2T§). 35.5 t.

76859. DTCso(A). Lot No. 30827 1972. 12/42 2T. 35.5 t.
62277–62304. MBSO. Lot No. 30804 1970. –/56. 49 t.
62287–62316. MBSO. Lot No. 30808 1970. –/56. 49 t.
62355–62425. MBSO. Lot No. 30816 1970. –/56. 49 t.
62430. MBSO. Lot No. 30829 1970. –/56. 49 t.
70967–70996. TSO. Lot No. 30809 1970–1971. –/72. 31.5t.
71035–71105. TSO. Lot No. 30817 1970. –/72. 31.5t.
71106. TSO. Lot No. 30830 1972. –/72. 31.5t.
71926–71928. TSO. Lot No. 30805 1970. –/72. 31.5t.
76571–76580. DTCso(B). Lot No. 30802 1970. 24/28 2T. 35 t.
76611–76640. DTCso(B). Lot No. 30807 1970. 24/28 2T. 35 t.
76788–76858. DTCso(B). Lot No. 30815 1970–1972. 24/28 2T. 35 t.
76860. DTCso(B). Lot No. 30828 1972. 18/36 2T. 35 t.

Notes: DTCso(A) were built with three first class compartments and one standard class compartment. On units marked † the three first class compartments have been declassified, whilst on units marked § all they have been converted to standard.
d Fitted with central door locking (ex-unit 1812).

Class 421/5. Phase 2 units. These sets are known as "Greyhound" units and are fitted with an additional stage of field weakening to improve the maximum attainable speed. This term is traditional on the lines of the former London & South Western railway, as it was formerly applied to their Class T9 4–4–0 express steam locomotives.

1301	**ST**	H	*SW*	FR	76595	62301	70981	76625
1302	**ST**	H	*SW*	FR	76584	62290	70970	76614
1303	**ST**	H	*SW*	FR	76581	62287	70967	76611
1304	**ST**	H	*SW*	FR	76583	62289	70969	76613
1305	**ST**	H	*SW*	FR	76717	62355	71035	76788
1306	**ST**	H	*SW*	FR	76723	62361	71041	76794
1307	**ST**	H	*SW*	FR	76586	62292	70972	76616
1308	**ST**	H	*SW*	FR	76627	62298	70978	76622
1309	**ST**	H	*SW*	FR	76594	62300	70980	76624
1310	**ST**	H	*SW*	FR	76567	62283	71926	76577
1311	**ST**	H	*SW*	FR	76561	62277	71927	76571
1312	**ST**	H	*SW*	FR	76562	62278	71928	76572
1313	**ST**	H	*SW*	FR	76596	62302	70982	76626
1314	**ST**	H	*SW*	FR	76588	62294	70974	76618
1315	**ST**	H	*SW*	FR	76608	62314	70994	76638
1316	**ST**	H	*SW*	FR	76585	62291	70971	76615
1317	**ST**	H	*SW*	FR	76597	62303	70983	76592
1318	**ST**	H	*SW*	FR	76590	62296	70976	76620
1319	**ST**	H	*SW*	FR	76591	62297	70977	76621
1320	**ST**	H	*SW*	FR	76593	62299	70979	76623
1321	**ST**	H	*SW*	FR	76589	62295	70975	76619
1322	**ST**	H	*SW*	FR	76587	62293	70973	76617

Former numbers of converted buffet cars:

71926 (69315) | 71927 (69330) | 71928 (69331)

Note: No new Lot Nos. were issued for the above conversions.

Class 421/8. 'Greyhound' units formed of former Class 422 units with the TRSB replaced by a Class 411/5 TSO.

1392	**ST**	P	*SW*	FR	76811	62378	70273	76740
1393	**ST**	P	*SW*	FR	76746	62384	70527	76817
1394	**ST**	P	*SW*	FR	76726	62364	70663	76797
1395	**ST**	P	*SW*	FR	76850	62417	70662	76779
1396	**ST**	P	*SW*	FR	76803	62370	70531	76732
1397	**ST**	P	*SW*	FR	76749	62387	70515	76820
1398	**ST**	P	*SW*	FR	76819	62386	70292	76748
1399	**ST**	P	*SW*	FR	76747	62385	70508	76818

Class 421/7. Phase 2 units rebuilt at Wessex Traincare/Alstom Eastleigh 1997–1998 for Brighton–Portsmouth "Coastway" line. Compartments opened out, first class seating replaced by standard with a TSO removed. Some units have had TSOs refitted in 2003.
SR designation: 3 Cop or 4 Cop.
Formation: DTSso(A)–MBSO–(TSO)–DTSso(B).
Diagram Numbers: EE245 + ED264 + EE245.
Accommodation: –/60 1T + –/56 1W + –/72 + –/60 1T.

1401	§	**CX**	P	*SC*	BI	76568	62284		76578
1403	§	**CX**	P	*SC*	BI	76563	62279	70703	76573
1404	§	**CX**	P	*SC*	BI	76602	62308		76632
1405	§	**CX**	P	*SC*	BI	76565	62281	70716	76575
1406	§	**CX**	P	*SC*	BI	76728	62366	70699	76799
1410	§	**CX**	P	*SC*	BI	76734	62372	70720	76805
1411	§	**CX**	P	*SC*	BI	76570	62286	70722	76580

Class 421/3. Phase 1 units.

1701		**U**	A	*SE*	RM	76087	62028	70706	76033
1704	†	**CX**	A	*SC*	BI	76092	62033	70711	76038
1705	†	**CX**	A		SU	76076	62017		76022
1707	†	**CX**	A		PY	76084	62025		76030
1708	†	**CX**	A	*SC*	BI	76110	62051	70729	76056
1709	†	**CX**	A		PY	76103	62044		76049
1710	†	**CX**	A	*SC*	BI	76078	62019	70697	76024
1711	§	**CX**	A	*SC*	BI	76114	62055	71766	76060
1712	†	**CX**	A	*SC*	BI	76079	62020	70698	76025
1713	§	**CX**	A	*SC*	BI	76128	62069	71767	76074
1714	†	**CX**	A	*SC*	BI	76077	62018	70696	76023
1717	†	**CX**	A	*SC*	BI	76083	62024	70702	76029
1719	†	**CX**	A	*SC*	BI	76116	62057	70719	76062
1720	†	**CX**	A	*SC*	BI	76098	62039	71769	76044
1721	§	**CX**	A	*SC*	BI	76090	62031	70709	76036
1722	§	**CX**	A	*SC*	BI	76106	62047	70725	76052
1724	†	**CX**	A	*SC*	BI	76120	62061	71770	76066
1725	†	**CX**	A	*SC*	BI	76088	62029	70707	76034
1726	§	**CX**	A		PY	76109	62050	70728	76055
1727	†	**CX**	A	*SC*	BI	76111	62052	70730	76057
1733	†	**CX**	A	*SC*	BI	76122	62063	71047	76068
1734	†	**U**	A	*SC*	BI	76063	62054	71044	76059

1735	†	**GA**	A	*SC*	BI	76117	62058	71050	76051
1736	†	**U**	A		PY	76124	62065	71052	76070
1737	†	**U**	A		PY	76121	62062	71058	76067
1738	†	**GA**	A		PY	76129	62064	71046	76069
1739	†	**CX**	A	*SC*	BI	76123	62070	71066	76075
1740	†	**GA**	A	*SC*	BI	76126	62067	71097	76072
1741	†	**CX**	A	*SC*	BI	76089	62030	70708	76035
1742		**U**	A	*SE*	RM	76086	62027	70705	76032
1743	†	**CX**	A	*SC*	BI	76118	62059	71065	76064
1744	†	**CX**	A	*SC*	BI	76127	62068	71064	76073
1745	§	**CX**	A		PY	76085	62026	70704	76031
1746	§	**CX**	A	*SC*	BI	76091	62032	70710	76037
1747	§	**CX**	A		PY	76093	62034	70712	76026
1748		**U**	A	*SE*	RM	76115	62056	71067	76061
1751	†	**CX**	A	*SC*	BI	76125	62066	71051	76071
1752	§	**CX**	A	*SC*	BI	76119	62060	70717	76065
1753	†	**CX**	A	*SC*	BI	76102	62043	70721	76048
Spare		**N**	A		PY		62053	71068	76058
Spare		**CX**	A		PY			70713	
Spare		**CX**	A		PY			70714	
Spare		**CX**	A		PY				76039

Class 421/4. Phase 2 units.

1801	†	**CX**	P	*SC*	BI	76848	62415	71095	76777
1802	†	**CX**	P	*SC*	BI	76754	62392	71072	76825
1803	†	**CX**	A	*SC*	BI	76780	62418	71098	76851
1804	†	**CX**	A	*SC*	BI	76778	62416	71096	76849
1805	†	**CX**	A	*SC*	BI	76782	62420	71100	76853
1806		**N**	H	*SE*	RM	76783	62421	71101	76854
1807		**N**	H	*SE*	RM	76784	62422	71102	76855
1808		**N**	H	*SE*	RM	76785	62423	71103	76856
1809		**N**	H	*SE*	RM	76786	62424	71104	76857
1810		**N**	H	*SE*	RM	76787	62425	71105	76858
1811		**N**	H	*SE*	RM	76781	62419	71099	76852
1813		**N**	H	*SE*	RM	76859	62430	71106	76860
1831	†	**CX**	A	*SC*	BI	76598	62304	70984	76628
1832	†	**CX**	A	*SC*	BI	76719	62357	71037	76790
1833	†	**CX**	A	*SC*	BI	76582	62288	70968	76612
1834	†	**CX**	A	*SC*	BI	76566	62282	70988	76576
1835	†	**CX**	A	*SC*	BI	76601	62307	70987	76631
1837	†	**CX**	A	*SC*	BI	76722	62360	71040	76793
1839		**N**	H	*SE*	RM	76607	62313	70993	76637
1840		**N**	H	*SE*	RM	76724	62362	71042	76795
1841		**N**	H	*SE*	RM	76603	62309	70989	76633
1842		**N**	H	*SE*	RM	76725	62363	71043	76796
1843		**N**	H	*SE*	RM	76731	62369	71049	76802
1845	†	**CX**	A	*SC*	BI	76599	62305	70985	76718
1846	†	**CX**	A	*SC*	BI	76737	62375	71055	76808
1847	†	**CX**	A	*SC*	BI	76600	62306	70986	76630
1848	†	**CX**	A	*SC*	BI	76605	62311	70991	76635
1850	†	**CX**	A		PY	76629	62356	71036	76789

1851	†	**U**	A	*SC*	BI	76721	62359	71039	76792
1853	†	**U**	A	*SC*	BI	76606	62312	70992	76636
1854	†	**GA**	A	*SC*	BI	76738	62376	71056	76809
1855	†	**CX**	A	*SC*	BI	76720	62358	71038	76791
1856	†	**GA**	A	*SC*	BI	76739	62377	71057	76810
1857	†	**GA**	A	*SC*	BI	76610	62316	70996	76640
1858	§	**GA**	A	*SC*	BI	76604	62310	70990	76634
1859	§	**GA**	A	*SC*	BI	76727	62365	71045	76798
1860	§	**GA**	A	*SC*	BI	76752	62390	71070	76823
1861	§	**GA**	A	*SC*	BI	76735	62373	71053	76806
1862	†	**GA**	A	*SC*	BI	76736	62374	71054	76807
1863	†	**CX**	A	*SC*	BI	76742	62380	71060	76813
1864	†	**CX**	A	*SC*	BI	76741	62379	71059	76812
1865	†	**CX**	A	*SC*	BI	76745	62383	71063	76639
1866	†	**CX**	A	*SC*	BI	76743	62381	71061	76814
1867	†	**CX**	A	*SC*	BI	76744	62382	71062	76815
1868	†	**CX**	A	*SC*	BI	76751	62389	71069	76822
1869	†	**CX**	A	*SC*	BI	76753	62391	71071	76804
1870		**CX**	H	*SE*	RM	76108	62409	71089	76842
1871		**N**	H	*SE*	RM	76756	62394	71074	76827
1872		**N**	H	*SE*	RM	76771	62396	71076	76829
1873		**N**	H	*SE*	RM	76759	62397	71077	76830
1874	†	**CX**	A	*SC*	BI	76755	62393	71073	76826
1876		**N**	H	*SE*	RM	76761	62399	71079	76832
1877		**N**	H	*SE*	RM	76763	62401	71081	76834
1878		**N**	H	*SE*	RM	76768	62406	71086	76839
1879		**N**	H	*SE*	RM	76760	62398	71078	76831
1880		**ST**	H	*SW*	FR	76770	62408	71088	76841
1881		**ST**	H	*SW*	FR	76762	62400	71080	76833
1882		**ST**	H	*SW*	FR	76765	62403	71083	76836
1883		**ST**	H	*SW*	FR	76764	62402	71082	76835
1884		**ST**	H	*SW*	FR	76767	62405	71085	76838
1885		**ST**	H	*SW*	FR	76769	62407	71087	76840
1886		**ST**	H	*SW*	FR	76772	62410	71090	76843
1887		**ST**	H	*SW*	FR	76766	62404	71084	76837
1888		**ST**	H	*SW*	FR	76773	62411	71091	76844
1889		**ST**	H	*SW*	FR	76774	62412	71092	76845
1890		**ST**	H	*SW*	FR	76775	62413	71093	76846
1891		**ST**	H	*SW*	FR	76776	62414	71094	76847
Spare	d	**N**	AM		ZG		62395		

Former numbers of converted buffet cars used in Phase 1 sets:

| 71766 (69303) | 71768 (69317) | 71769 (69305) | 71770 (69308) |
| 71767 (69314) | | | |

Note: No new lot numbers were issued for the above conversions
Class 421/9. Phase 1 units fitted with ex-Class 432 Mark 6 motor bogies.

1901	†	**CX**	P	*SC*	BI	76082	62023	70701	76028
1903	†	**CX**	A		PY	76081	62022	70700	76027
1904	†	**CX**	A	*SC*	BI	76107	62048	70726	76053
1905	§	**CX**	A	*SC*	BI	76099	62040	70718	76045

1906	† **CX**	A	*SC*	BI	76105	62046	70724	76113
1907	† **CX**	A	*SC*	BI	76104	62045	70723	76050
1908	† **GA**	A	*SC*	BI	76096	62037	70715	76042

CLASS 423   BR

Outer suburban units. Facelifted with fluorescent lighting.

SR designation: 4 Vep.
Formation: DTCSO(A)–MBSO–TSO–DTCSO(B).
Construction: Steel.   **Doors:** Slam.
Gangways: Throughout.   **Electrical Equipment:** 1966-type.
Traction Motors: Four EE507 of 185 kW. **Couplers:** Buckeye.
Bogies: Two Mk. 4 motor bogies (MBSO). B5 (SR) bogies (trailer cars).
Maximum Speed: 90 m.p.h.   **Dimensions:** 20.18 x 2.82 m.
Seating Layout: 1: Compartments, 2: 3+2 facing or compartments.
Braking: Tread brakes.
Multiple Working: Within class and with Classes 411, 412, 421, 438 and locos of
Classes 33/1 and 73.

62121–62140. MBSO. Lot No. 30760 Derby 1967. –/76. 49 t.
62182–62216. MBSO. Lot No. 30773 York 1967–1968. –/76. 49 t.
62217–62266. MBSO. Lot No. 30794 York 1968–1969. –/76. 49 t.
62267–62276. MBSO. Lot No. 30800 York 1970. –/76. 49 t.
62317–62354. MBSO. Lot No. 30813 York 1970–1973. –/76. 49 t.
62435–62475. MBSO. Lot No. 30851 York 1973–1974. –/76. 49 t.
70781–70800. TSO. Lot No. 30759 Derby 1967. –/98. 31.5 t.
70872–70906. TSO. Lot No. 30772 York 1967–1968. –/98. 31.5 t.
70907–70956. TSO. Lot No. 30793 York 1968–1969. –/98. 31.5 t.
70957–70966. TSO. Lot No. 30801 York 1970. –/98. 31.5 t.
70997–71034. TSO. Lot No. 30812 York 1970–1973. –/98. 31.5 t.
71115–71155. TSO. Lot No. 30852 York 1973–1974. –/98. 31.5 t.
76230–76269. DTCso Lot No. 30758 York 1967. 18/46 1T. 35 t.
76275. DTSO (Class 438). Lot No. 30764 York 1966. –/64 1T. 32 t. (Converted
from hauled TSO 3929). Now in unit 3582.
76333–76402. DTCso. Lot No. 30771 York 1967–1968. 18/46 1T. 35 t.
76441–76540. DTCso. Lot No. 30792 York 1968–1969. 18/46 1T. 35 t.
76541–76560. DTCso. Lot No. 30799 York 1970. 18/46 1T. 35 t.
76641–76716. DTCso. Lot No. 30811 York 1970–1973. 18/46 1T. 35 t.
76861–76942. DTCso. Lot No. 30853 York 1973–1974. 18/46 1T. 35 t.

Class 423/1. Standard units.

3401	**ST**	H	*SW*	WD	76871	62276	70781	76872
3402	**ST**	H	*SW*	WD	76233	62123	70782	76232
3403	**CX**	H	*SC*	BI	76234	62254	70783	76235
3404	**ST**	H	*SW*	WD	76378	62261	70894	76236
3405	**ST**	H	*SW*	WD	76239	62271	70785	76238
3406	**ST**	H	*SW*	WD	76241	62130	70786	76240
3407	**ST**	H	*SW*	WD	76243	62348	70787	76242
3408	**ST**	H	*SW*	WD	76244	62435	70788	76245
3409	**ST**	H	*SW*	WD	76246	62239	70789	76247

3410	ST	H	SW	WD	76369	62442	70790	76249
3411	ST	H	SW	WD	76250	62342	70791	76251
3412	CX	A	SE	RM	76252	62340	70792	76253
3413	ST	H	SW	WD	76255	62441	70793	76254
3414	ST	H	SW	WD	76257	62446	70794	76248
3415	N	H	SW	WD	76258	62462	70795	76259
3416	CX	A	SE	RM	76261	62451	70796	76260
3417	ST	H	SW	WD	76262	62236	70797	76263
3418	ST	H	SW	WD	76265	62133	70875	76264
3419	ST	H	SW	WD	76267	62354	70799	76266
3420	ST	H	SW	WD	76269	62349	70800	76268
3421	CX	A	SE	RM	76889	62449	71129	76890
3422	CX	A	SE	RM	76372	62201	70891	76371
3423	CX	A	SE	RM	76452	62222	70912	76451
3424	CX	A	SE	RM	76354	62185	70882	76353
3425	ST	H	SW	WD	76338	62192	70874	76358
3426	ST	H	SW	WD	76386	62208	70898	76385
3427	ST	H	SW	WD	76374	62184	70892	76373
3428	ST	H	SW	WD	76231	62223	70913	76453
3429	ST	H	SW	WD	76334	62202	70872	76333
3430	ST	H	SW	WD	76348	62189	70879	76347
3431	ST	H	SW	WD	76458	62182	70915	76457
3432	ST	H	SW	WD	76400	62225	70905	76399
3433	ST	H	SW	WD	76444	62215	70908	76443
3434	ST	H	SW	WD	76462	62218	70917	76461
3436	CX	P	SC	BI	76350	62190	70880	76349
3437	CX	P	SC	BI	76346	62186	70878	76345
3445	CX	A	SE	RM	76450	62242	70911	76449
3446	CX	A	SE	RM	76532	62243	70952	76531
3447	CX	A	SE	RM	76380	62199	70895	76379
3448	CX	A	SE	RM	76376	62221	70886	76375
3449	CX	A	SE	RM	76336	62205	70873	76335
3450	CX	A	SE	RM	76460	62203	70916	76459
3451	CX	A	SE	RM	76488	62240	70930	76487
3452	CX	A	SE	RM	76340	62183	71021	76690
3453	CX	A	SE	RM	76382	62226	70896	76381
3454	CX	A	SE	RM	76390	62200	70798	76389
3455	ST	H	SW	WD	76388	62206	70899	76387
3456	ST	H	SW	WD	76455	62210	70914	76230
3457	ST	H	SW	WD	76392	62197	70901	76391
3458	ST	H	SW	WD	76394	62209	70902	76393
3459	ST	H	SW	WD	76396	62224	70903	76395
3466	ST	H	SW	WD	76464	62214	70918	76463
3467	ST	H	SW	WD	76446	62217	70909	76445
3468	ST	H	SW	WD	76448	62267	70910	76447
3469	ST	H	SW	WD	76546	62219	70959	76545
3470	ST	H	SW	WD	76496	62220	70934	76495
3471	CX	A	SE	RM	76498	62269	70935	76497
3472	CX	A	SE	RM	76500	62244	70936	76499
3473	CX	A	SE	RM	76502	62245	70937	76339
3474	CX	A	SE	RM	76504	62246	70938	76503

3475	**CX**	A	*SE*	RM	76552	62270	70962	76551
3479	**CX**	H	*SC*	BI	76655	62272	71004	76656
3480	**ST**	H	*SW*	WD	76474	62323	70923	76473
3481	**ST**	H	*SW*	WD	76647	62324	70900	76648
3482	**CX**	H	*SC*	BI	76657	62320	71005	76658
3483	**CX**	H	*SC*	BI	76661	62233	71007	76662
3484	**CX**	H	*SC*	BI	76476	62325	70924	76475
3485	**CX**	H	*SC*	BI	76508	62327	70940	76507
3486	**CX**	H	*SC*	BI	76478	62234	70925	76477
3487	**CX**	A	*SE*	RM	76645	62250	70941	76509
3488	**CX**	H	*SC*	BI	76663	62235	71008	76664
3489	**CX**	H	*SC*	BI	76665	62251	71009	76666
3490	**CX**	H	*SC*	BI	76695	62328	71024	76696
3491	**CX**	A	*SE*	RM	76337	62436	70927	76481
3492	**CX**	A	*SE*	RM	76667	62344	71010	76668
3493	**CX**	A	*SE*	RM	76669	62237	71011	76670
3494	**CX**	A	*SE*	RM	76675	62330	71014	76676
3495	**CX**	A	*SE*	RM	76699	62331	71026	76700
3496	**CX**	A	*SE*	RM	76673	62334	71013	76674
3497	**CX**	A	*SE*	RM	76671	62346	71012	76672
3498	**CX**	A	*SE*	RM	76701	62333	71027	76702
3499	**CX**	A	*SE*	RM	76901	62347	71135	76902
3500	**CX**	A	*SE*	RM	76470	62455	70921	76469
3501	**CX**	P	*SC*	BI	76512	62332	70942	76511
3505	**CX**	P		BI	76472	62352	70922	76471
3508	**ST**	H	*SW*	WD	76643	62273	70998	76644
3509	**ST**	H	*SW*	WD	76560	62275	70966	76559
3510	**ST**	H	*SW*	WD	76641	62318	70997	76642
3511	**CX**	A	*SE*	RM	76893	62135	70999	76646
3512	**CX**	P	*SC*	BI	76679	62337	71016	76680
3514	**GA**	P	*SC*	BI	76683	62136	71018	76684
3515	**CX**	P	*SC*	BI	76544	62319	70958	76543
3516	**ST**	H	*SW*	WD	76693	62268	71023	76694
3517	**CX**	P	*SC*	BI	76685	62338	71019	76686
3519	**ST**	H	*SW*	WD	76556	62274	70964	76555
3520	**ST**	H	*SW*	WD	76697	62131	71025	76698
3521	**CX**	A	*SE*	RM	76484	62345	70928	76483
3523	**CX**	H	*SC*	BI	76651	62139	71002	76652
3524	**CX**	H	*SC*	BI	76466	62322	70919	76370
3529	**CX**	H	*SC*	BI	76659	62257	71006	76660
3530	**CX**	H	*SC*	BI	76468	62256	70920	76467
3531	**CX**	H	*SC*	BI	76649	62230	71001	76650
3535	**CX**	P	*SC*	BI	76677	62335	71015	76678
3536	**ST**	H	*SW*	WD	76384	62207	70897	76383
3539	**ST**	H	*SW*	WD	76862	62122	71115	76861
3540	**ST**	H	*SW*	WD	76863	62128	71116	76864
3542	**ST**	H	*SW*	WD	76480	62127	70926	76479
3543	**N**	A	*SE*	RM	76899	62137	71134	76900
3544	**CX**	A	*SE*	RM	76892	62454	71131	76894
3545	**CX**	A	*SE*	RM	76875	62121	71122	76876
3546	**CX**	P	*SC*	BI	76687	62339	71020	76688

3547	CX	A	SE	RM	76895	62126	71132	76896
3548	CX	A	SE	RM	76903	62452	71136	76904
3549	CX	P	SC	BI	76707	62132	71030	76708
3551	CX	P	SC	BI	76465	62456	71033	76714
3552	ST	H	SW	WD	76715	62353	71034	76716
3553	CX	A	SE	RM	76913	62241	71141	76914
3554	CX	A	SE	RM	76905	62461	71137	76906
3555	ST	H	SW	WD	76865	62140	71117	76866
3556	CX	A	SE	RM	76885	62457	71127	76886
3557	ST	H	SW	WD	76869	62437	71119	76870
3558	ST	H	SW	WD	76352	62447	70881	76351
3559	ST	H	SW	WD	76486	62439	70929	76485
3560	CX	A	SE	RM	76897	62191	71133	76898
3561	ST	H	SW	WD	76867	62453	71118	76868
3562	CX	A	SE	RM	76907	62129	71138	76908
3563	ST	H	SW	WD	76873	62438	71121	76874
3564	CX	A	SE	RM	76883	62458	71126	76884
3565	CX	A	SE	RM	76877	62134	71123	76878
3566	CX	A	SE	RM	76915	62443	71142	76916
3568	CX	A	SE	RM	76887	62440	71128	76888
3569	ST	H	SW	WD	76344	62448	70877	76343
3570	CX	A	SE	RM	76909	62187	71139	76910
3571	CX	A	SE	RM	76927	62463	71148	76928
3572	CX	A	SE	RM	76879	62468	71124	76880
3573	CX	A	SE	RM	76919	62444	71144	76920
3574	CX	A	SE	RM	76929	62464	71149	76930
3575	CX	A	SE	RM	76931	62469	71150	76932
3576	ST	H	SW	WD	76362	62196	70890	76361
3577	CX	A	SE	RM	76933	62459	71151	76934
3578	ST	H	SW	WD	76356	62193	70883	76355
3579	CX	A	SE	RM	76935	62471	71152	76936
3580	ST	H	SW	WD	76359	62195	70885	76360
3581	ST	H	SW	WD	76366	62198	70888	76365
3582	CX	A	SE	RM	76891	62472	71130	76275
3583	CX	A	SE	RM	76937	62450	71153	76938
3584	CX	A	SE	RM	76881	62473	71125	76882
3585	CX	A	SE	RM	76939	62445	71154	76940
3586	CX	A	SE	RM	76921	62474	71145	76922
3587	CX	A	SE	RM	76925	62465	71147	76926
3588	CX	A	SE	RM	76923	62467	71146	76924
3589	CX	A	SE	RM	76911	62466	71140	76912
3590	CX	A	SE	RM	76941	62460	71155	76942
3591	CX	A	SE	RM	76917	62475	71143	76918
3801	CX	P	SE	RM	76522	62229	70947	76521
3802	CX	P	SE	RM	76534	62188	70953	76533
3803	CX	P	SE	RM	76494	62263	70933	76493
3804	CX	P	SE	RM	76368	62204	70889	76367
3805	CX	P	SE	RM	76540	62211	70956	76539
3806	CX	P	SE	RM	76538	62212	70955	76537
3807	CX	P	SE	RM	76542	62264	70957	76541
3808	CX	P	SE	RM	76550	62248	70961	76549

3809	**N**	P	*SW*	WD	76516	62253	70944	76515
3810	**N**	P	*SW*	WD	76709	62252	71031	76710
3811	**N**	P	*SW*	WD	76514	62249	70943	76513
3812	**N**	ST	*SW*	WD	76703	62238	71028	76704
Spare	**N**	H		WD		62470		

Class 423/2. Reformed South Central units (converted from 4 Vops (see below) and 4 Veps). Programme ongoing as this book went to press –see **entrain** for developments.

SR designation: 4 Vip.
Formation: DTCso–MBSO–TSO–DTSso.
DTSso seat –/70 1T.

3813	**CX**	P	*SC*	BI	76653	62125	71003	76342
3814	**CX**	P	*SC*	BI	76654	62228	70876	76341
3815								
3816								
3817								
3818								
3819								
3820								
3821	**CX**	P	*SC*	BI	76711	62262	70951	76530
3822	**CX**	P	*SC*	BI	76529	62351	71032	76712
3823								
3824								
3825								
3826								
3827								
3828								
3829								
3830								
3831								
3832								
3833								
3834								
3835								
3836								
3837								
3838								
3839								
3840								
3841	**CX**	P	*SC*	BI	76520	62326	70946	76689
3842	**CX**	P	*SC*	BI	76519	62343	70887	76363
3843	**CX**	P	*SC*	BI	76681	62350	70931	76489
3844	**CX**	P	*SC*	BI	76490	62231	71017	76682

Class 423/2. Units converted for "South London Metro" service.

SR designation: 4 Vop.
Formation: DTSso(A)–MBSO–TSO–DTSso(B).
DTSso seat –/70 1T.

3901	CX	P	SC	Bl	76402	62227	70906	76401
3902	CX	P	SC	Bl	76364	62260	70949	76525
3903	CX	P	SC	Bl	76536	62213	70954	76535
3904	CX	P	SC	Bl	76691	62336	71022	76692
3905	CX	P	SC	Bl	76398	62266	70904	76397
3907	CX	P	SC	Bl	76506	62259	70939	76505
3908	CX	P	SC	Bl	76442	62265	70907	76441
3909	CX	P	SC	Bl	76705	62341	71029	76706
3911	CX	P	SC	Bl	76548	62247	70960	76547
3912	CX	P	SC	Bl	76492	62216	70932	76491
3915	CX	P	SC	Bl	76524	62255	70948	76523
3916	CX	P	SC	Bl	76518	62258	70945	76517
3917	CX	P	SC	Bl	76558	62232	70965	76557
3918	CX	P	SC	Bl	76528	62321	70950	76527
3919	CX	P	SC	Bl	76554	62317	70963	76553

CLASS 442 WESSEX EXPRESS   BREL DERBY

Stock built for Waterloo–Bournemouth–Weymouth service. Now also used on certain Portsmouth Harbour services. Can be hauled and heated by any ETH fitted locomotive.

SR designation: 5 Wes.
Formation: DTFso–TSO(A)–MBRSM–TSO(B)–DTSO.
Construction: Steel.   **Doors:** Sliding plug.
Gangways: Throughout.   **Electrical Equipment:** 1986-type.
Traction Motors: Four EE546 of 300 kW recovered from class 432.
Bogies: Two BREL P7 motor bogies (MBSO). T4 bogies (trailer cars).
Maximum Speed: 100 m.p.h.   **Couplers:** Buckeye.
Seating Layout: 1: 2+2 facing/compartments, 2: 2+2 facing/unidirectional.
Dimensions: 23.15/23.00 x 2.74 m.   **Braking:** Disc brakes.
Heating & Ventilation: Air conditioning.
Multiple Working: Within class and with Classes 411, 412, 423, 438 and locos of Classes 33/1 and 73 in emergency.

DTFso. Lot No. 31030 Derby 1988–1989. 50/– 1T. (36 in six compartments and 14 in one saloon). Public Telephone. 38.2 t.
TSO (A). Lot No. 31032 Derby 1988–1989. –/82 2T. 35.3 t.
MBRBS. Lot No. 31034 Derby 1988–1989. Modified Adtranz Crewe 1998. –/52 1W. 54.9 t.
TSO (B). Lot No. 31033 Derby 1988–1989. –/78 2T 1W. 35.4 t.
DTSO. Lot No. 31031 Derby 1988–1989. –/78 1T. 35.7 t.

2401	SW	A	SW	BM	77382	71818	62937	71842	77406
2402	SW	A	SW	BM	77383	71819	62938	71843	77407
2403	SW	A	SW	BM	77384	71820	62941	71844	77408
2404	SW	A	SW	BM	77385	71821	62939	71845	77409
2405	SW	A	SW	BM	77386	71822	62944	71846	77410
2406	SW	A	SW	BM	77389	71823	62942	71847	77411
2407	SW	A	SW	BM	77388	71824	62943	71848	77412
2408	SW	A	SW	BM	77387	71825	62945	71849	77413

2409	**SW**	A SW	BM	77390	71826	62946	71850	77414
2410	**SW**	A SW	BM	77391	71827	62948	71851	77415
2411	**SW**	A SW	BM	77392	71828	62940	71858	77422
2412	**SW**	A SW	BM	77393	71829	62947	71853	77417
2413	**SW**	A SW	BM	77394	71830	62949	71854	77418
2414	**SW**	A SW	BM	77395	71831	62950	71855	77419
2415	**SW**	A SW	BM	77396	71832	62951	71856	77420
2416	**SW**	A SW	BM	77397	71833	62952	71857	77421
2417	**SW**	A SW	BM	77398	71834	62953	71852	77416
2418	**SW**	A SW	BM	77399	71835	62954	71859	77423
2419	**SW**	A SW	BM	77400	71836	62955	71860	77424
2420	**SW**	A SW	BM	77401	71837	62956	71861	77425
2421	**SW**	A SW	BM	77402	71838	62957	71862	77426
2422	**SW**	A SW	BM	77403	71839	62958	71863	77427
2423	**SW**	A SW	BM	77404	71840	62959	71864	77428
2424	**SW**	A SW	BM	77405	71841	62960	71865	77429

Names (carried on MBRSM):

2401	BEAULIEU
2402	COUNTY OF HAMPSHIRE
2403	THE NEW FOREST
2404	BOROUGH OF WOKING
2405	CITY OF PORTSMOUTH
2406	VICTORY
2407	THOMAS HARDY
2408	COUNTY OF DORSET
2409	BOURNEMOUTH ORCHESTRAS
2410	MERIDIAN TONIGHT
2411	THE RAILWAY CHILDREN
2412	SPECIAL OLYMPICS
2415	MARY ROSE
2416	MUM IN A MILLION 1997, DOREEN SCANLON
2417	WOKING HOMES
2418	WESSEX CANCER TRUST
2419	BBC SOUTH TODAY
2420	CITY OF SOUTHAMPTON
2422	OPERATION OVERLORD
2423	COUNTY OF SURREY
2424	GERRY NEWSON

CLASS 444   DESIRO UK   SIEMENS

New 5-car express units for South West Trains.
Formation: DMCO–TSO–TSO–TSRMB–DMSO.
Construction: Aluminium.   **Doors:** Single-leaf sliding plug.
Traction Motors: 4 Siemens 1TB2016-0GB02 asynchronous of 250 kW.
Gangways: Throughout.   **Bogies:** SGP SF5000.
Couplers: Dellner 12.   **Maximum Speed:** 100 m.p.h.
Seating Layout: 1: 2+1 facing/unidirectional, 2: 2+2 facing/unidirectional.
Dimensions: 23.57 m x 2.74 m.
Braking: Disc and rheostatic.

Multiple Working: Within class and with Class 450.

DMSO. Siemens Wien 2003–2004. –/76. 52.0 t.
TSO. Siemens Wien 2003–2004. –/76 1T. 41.0 t.
TSORMB. Siemens Wien 2003–2004. –/47 2W 1T 1TD. 42.0 t.
DMCO. Siemens Wien 2003–2004. 35/24. 52.0 t.

444 001	**SW**	A		63801	67101	67151	67201	63851
444 002	**SW**	A		63802	67102	67152	67202	63852
444 003	**SW**	A		63803	67103	67153	67203	63853
444 004	**SW**	A		63804	67104	67154	67204	63854
444 005	**SW**	A		63805	67105	67155	67205	63855
444 006	**SW**	A		63806	67106	67156	67206	63856
444 007	**SW**	A		63807	67107	67157	67207	63857
444 008	**SW**	A		63808	67108	67158	67208	63858
444 009	**SW**	A		63809	67109	67159	67209	63859
444 010	**SW**	A		63810	67110	67160	67210	63860
444 011	**SW**	A	NT	63811	67111	67161	67211	63861
444 012	**SW**	A		63812	67112	67162	67212	63862
444 013	**SW**	A		63813	67113	67163	67213	63863
444 014	**SW**	A		63814	67114	67164	67214	63864
444 015	**SW**	A		63815	67115	67165	67215	63865
444 016	**SW**	A		63816	67116	67166	67216	63866
444 017	**SW**	A		63817	67117	67167	67217	63867
444 018	**SW**	A		63818	67118	67168	67218	63868
444 019	**SW**	A		63819	67119	67169	67219	63869
444 020	**SW**	A		63820	67120	67170	67220	63870
444 021	**SW**	A		63821	67121	67171	67221	63871
444 022	**SW**	A		63822	67122	67172	67222	63872
444 023	**SW**	A		63823	67123	67173	67223	63873
444 024	**SW**	A		63824	67124	67174	67224	63874
444 025	**SW**	A		63825	67125	67175	67225	63875
444 026	**SW**	A		63826	67126	67176	67226	63876
444 027	**SW**	A		63827	67127	67177	67227	63877
444 028	**SW**	A		63828	67128	67178	67228	63878
444 029	**SW**	A		63829	67129	67179	67229	63879
444 030	**SW**	A		63830	67130	67180	67230	63880
444 031	**SW**	A		63831	67131	67181	67231	63881
444 032	**SW**	A		63832	67132	67182	67232	63882
444 033	**SW**	A		63833	67133	67183	67233	63883
444 034	**SW**	A		63834	67134	67184	67234	63884
444 035	**SW**	A		63835	67135	67185	67235	63885
444 036	**SW**	A		63836	67136	67186	67236	63886
444 037	**SW**	A		63837	67137	67187	67237	63887
444 038	**SW**	A		63838	67138	67188	67238	63888
444 039	**SW**	A		63839	67139	67189	67239	63889
444 040	**SW**	A		63840	67140	67190	67240	63890
444 041	**SW**	A		63841	67141	67191	67241	63891
444 042	**SW**	A		63842	67142	67192	67242	63892
444 043	**SW**	A		63843	67143	67193	67243	63893
444 044	**SW**	A		63844	67144	67194	67244	63894
444 045	**SW**	A		63845	67145	67195	67245	63895

CLASS 450   DESIRO UK   SIEMENS

New 4-car suburban units now being delivered for South West Trains. Original order for 5-car Class 450s has now been cancelled.

Formations: DMSO–TCO–TSO–DMSO.
Construction: Aluminium.   **Doors:** Sliding plug.
Traction Motors: 4 Siemens 1TB2016-0GB02 asynchronous of 250 kW.
Gangways: Throughout.   **Bogies:** SGP SF5000.
Couplers: Dellner 12.   **Maximum Speed:** 100 m.p.h.
Seating Layout: 1: 2+2 facing/unidirectional, 2: 3+2 facing/unidirectional.
Dimensions: 20.40 x 2.79 m.
Braking: Disc and rheostatic.
Multiple Working: Within class and with Class 444.

DMSO(A). Siemens Uerdingen/Wien 2002–2004. –/70. 46.0 t.
TCO. Siemens Uerdingen/Wien 2002–2004. 24/36 1T. 35.0 t.
TSO. Siemens Uerdingen/Wien 2002–2004. –/70 2W 1TD. 35.0 t.
DMSO(B). Siemens Uerdingen/Wien 2002–2004. –/70. 46.0 t.

450 001	**SD**	A			63201	64201	68101	63601
450 002	**SD**	A			63202	64202	68102	63602
450 003	**SD**	A			63203	64203	68103	63603
450 004	**SD**	A			63204	64204	68104	63604
450 005	**SD**	A			63205	64205	68105	63605
450 006	**SD**	A		NT	63206	64206	68106	63606
450 007	**SD**	A		NT	63207	64207	68107	63607
450 008	**SD**	A		NT	63208	64208	68108	63608
450 009	**SD**	A	*SW*	NT	63209	64209	68109	63609
450 010	**SD**	A		NT	63210	64210	68110	63610
450 011	**SD**	A		NT	63211	64211	68111	63611
450 012	**SD**	A			63212	64212	68112	63612
450 013	**SD**	A	*SW*	NT	63213	64213	68113	63613
450 014	**SD**	A			63214	64214	68114	63614
450 015	**SD**	A	*SW*	NT	63215	64215	68115	63615	DESIRO
450 016	**SD**	A	*SW*	NT	63216	64216	68116	63616
450 017	**SD**	A			63217	64217	68117	63617
450 018	**SD**	A	*SW*	NT	63218	64218	68118	63618
450 019	**SD**	A	*SW*	NT	63219	64219	68119	63619
450 020	**SD**	A			63220	64220	68120	63620
450 021	**SD**	A	*SW*	NT	63221	64221	68121	63621
450 022	**SD**	A			63222	64222	68122	63622
450 023	**SD**	A	*SW*	NT	63223	64223	68123	63623
450 024	**SD**	A	*SW*	NT	63224	64224	68124	63624
450 025	**SD**	A	*SW*	NT	63225	64225	68125	63625
450 026	**SD**	A	*SW*	NT	63226	64226	68126	63626
450 027	**SD**	A	*SW*	NT	63227	64227	68127	63627
450 028	**SD**	A		NT	63228	64228	68128	63628
450 029	**SD**	A	*SW*	NT	63229	64229	68129	63629
450 030	**SD**	A			63230	64230	68130	63630
450 031	**SD**	A			63231	64231	68131	63631
450 032	**SD**	A			63232	64232	68132	63632

450 033	**SD**	A	*SW*	NT	63233	64233	68133	63633
450 034	**SD**	A			63234	64234	68134	63634
450 035	**SD**	A			63235	64235	68135	63635
450 036	**SD**	A			63236	64236	68136	63636
450 037	**SD**	A			63237	64237	68137	63637
450 038	**SD**	A	*SW*	NT	63238	64238	68138	63638
450 039	**SD**	A			63239	64239	68139	63639
450 040	**SD**	A			63240	64240	68140	63640
450 041	**SD**	A			63241	64241	68141	63641
450 042	**SD**	A			63242	64242	68142	63642
450 043	**SD**	A			63243	64243	68143	63643
450 044	**SD**	A			63244	64244	68144	63644
450 045	**SD**	A			63245	64245	68145	63645
450 046	**SD**	A			63246	64246	68146	63646
450 047	**SD**	A			63247	64247	68147	63647
450 048	**SD**	A			63248	64248	68148	63648
450 049	**SD**	A			63249	64249	68149	63649
450 050	**SD**	A			63250	64250	68150	63650
450 051	**SD**	A			63251	64251	68151	63651
450 052	**SD**	A			63252	64252	68152	63652
450 053	**SD**	A			63253	64253	68153	63653
450 054	**SD**	A			63254	64254	68154	63654
450 055	**SD**	A			63255	64255	68155	63655
450 056	**SD**	A			63256	64256	68156	63656
450 057	**SD**	A			63257	64257	68157	63657
450 058	**SD**	A			63258	64258	68158	63658
450 059	**SD**	A			63259	64259	68159	63659
450 060	**SD**	A			63260	64260	68160	63660
450 061	**SD**	A			63261	64261	68161	63661
450 062	**SD**	A			63262	64262	68162	63662
450 063	**SD**	A			63263	64263	68163	63663
450 064	**SD**	A			63264	64264	68164	63664
450 065	**SD**	A			63265	64265	68165	63665
450 066	**SD**	A			63266	64266	68166	63666
450 067	**SD**	A			63267	64267	68167	63667
450 068	**SD**	A			63268	64268	68168	63668
450 069	**SD**	A			63269	64269	68169	63669
450 070	**SD**	A			63270	64270	68170	63670
450 071	**SD**	A			63271	64271	68171	63671
450 072	**SD**	A			63272	64272	68172	63672
450 073	**SD**	A			63273	64273	68173	63673
450 074	**SD**	A			63274	64274	68174	63674
450 075	**SD**	A			63275	64275	68175	63675
450 076	**SD**	A			63276	64276	68176	63676
450 077	**SD**	A			63277	64277	68177	63677
450 078	**SD**	A			63278	64278	68178	63678
450 079	**SD**	A			63279	64279	68179	63679
450 080	**SD**	A			63280	64280	68180	63680
450 081	**SD**	A			63281	64281	68181	63681
450 082	**SD**	A			63282	64282	68182	63682
450 083	**SD**	A			63283	64283	68183	63683

450 084	**SD**	A	63284	64284	68184	63684
450 085	**SD**	A	63285	64285	68185	63685
450 086	**SD**	A	63286	64286	68186	63686
450 087	**SD**	A	63287	64287	68187	63687
450 088	**SD**	A	63288	64288	68188	63688
450 089	**SD**	A	63289	64289	68189	63689
450 090	**SD**	A	63290	64290	68190	63690
450 091	**SD**	A	63291	64291	68191	63691
450 092	**SD**	A	63292	64292	68192	63692
450 093	**SD**	A	63293	64293	68193	63693
450 094	**SD**	A	63294	64294	68194	63694
450 095	**SD**	A	63295	64295	68195	63695
450 096	**SD**	A	63296	64296	68196	63696
450 097	**SD**	A	63297	64297	68197	63697
450 098	**SD**	A	63298	64298	68198	63698
450 099	**SD**	A	63299	64299	68199	63699
450 100	**SD**	A	63300	64300	68200	63700
450 101	**SD**	A	63701	66801	66851	63751
450 102	**SD**	A	63702	66802	66852	63752
450 103	**SD**	A	63703	66803	66853	63753
450 104	**SD**	A	63704	66804	66854	63754
450 105	**SD**	A	63705	66805	66855	63755
450 106	**SD**	A	63706	66806	66856	63756
450 107	**SD**	A	63707	66807	66857	63757
450 108	**SD**	A	63708	66808	66858	63758
450 109	**SD**	A	63709	66809	66859	63759
450 110	**SD**	A	63710	66810	66860	63760

CLASS 455   BR YORK

South West Trains/South Central inner suburban units.

Formation: DTSO–MSO–TSO–DTSO.
Construction: Steel. Class 455/7 TSO have a steel underframe and an aluminium alloy body & roof.
Doors: Sliding.
Gangways: Throughout.   **Electrical Equipment:** 1966-type.
Traction Motors: Four GEC507-20J of 185 kW.
Bogies: P7 (motor) and T3 (455/8 & 455/9) BX1 (455/7) trailer.
Couplers: Tightlock.
Maximum Speed: 75 m.p.h.   **Seating Layout:** 3+2 facing.
Dimensions: 20.18 x 2.82 m.   **Braking:** Disc brakes.
Heating & Ventilation: Various.
Multiple Working: Within class and with Class 456.

Class 455/7. Second series with TSOs originally in Class 508. Pressure heating and ventilation.

DTSO. Lot No. 30976 1984–1985. –/74. 29.5 t.
MSO. Lot No. 30975 1984–1985. –/84. 45 t.
TSO. Lot No. 30944 1977–1980. –/86. 25.48 t.

5701	**ST**	P	*SW*	WD	77727	62783	71545	77728
5702	**ST**	P	*SW*	WD	77729	62784	71547	77730
5703	**ST**	P	*SW*	WD	77731	62785	71540	77732
5704	**ST**	P	*SW*	WD	77733	62786	71548	77734
5705	**N**	P	*SW*	WD	77735	62787	71565	77736
5706	**ST**	P	*SW*	WD	77737	62788	71534	77738
5707	**N**	P	*SW*	WD	77739	62789	71536	77740
5708	**ST**	P	*SW*	WD	77741	62790	71560	77742
5709	**N**	P	*SW*	WD	77743	62791	71532	77744
5710	**N**	P	*SW*	WD	77745	62792	71566	77746
5711	**N**	P	*SW*	WD	77747	62793	71542	77748
5712	**N**	P	*SW*	WD	77749	62794	71546	77750
5713	**ST**	P	*SW*	WD	77751	62795	71567	77752
5714	**ST**	P	*SW*	WD	77753	62796	71539	77754
5715	**ST**	P	*SW*	WD	77755	62797	71535	77756
5716	**ST**	P	*SW*	WD	77757	62798	71564	77758
5717	**N**	P	*SW*	WD	77759	62799	71528	77760
5718	**ST**	P	*SW*	WD	77761	62800	71557	77762
5719	**ST**	P	*SW*	WD	77763	62801	71558	77764
5720	**ST**	P	*SW*	WD	77765	62802	71568	77766
5721	**ST**	P	*SW*	WD	77767	62803	71553	77768
5722	**ST**	P	*SW*	WD	77769	62804	71533	77770
5723	**ST**	P	*SW*	WD	77771	62805	71526	77772
5724	**ST**	P	*SW*	WD	77773	62806	71561	77774
5725	**ST**	P	*SW*	WD	77775	62807	71541	77776
5726	**ST**	P	*SW*	WD	77777	62808	71556	77778
5727	**ST**	P	*SW*	WD	77779	62809	71562	77780
5728	**ST**	P	*SW*	WD	77781	62810	71527	77782
5729	**ST**	P	*SW*	WD	77783	62811	71550	77784
5730	**ST**	P	*SW*	WD	77785	62812	71551	77786
5731	**ST**	P	*SW*	WD	77787	62813	71555	77788
5732	**ST**	P	*SW*	WD	77789	62814	71552	77790
5733	**ST**	P	*SW*	WD	77791	62815	71549	77792
5734	**ST**	P	*SW*	WD	77793	62816	71531	77794
5735	**ST**	P	*SW*	WD	77795	62817	71563	77796
5736	**ST**	P	*SW*	WD	77797	62818	71554	77798
5737	**ST**	P	*SW*	WD	77799	62819	71544	77800
5738	**ST**	P	*SW*	WD	77801	62820	71529	77802
5739	**ST**	P	*SW*	WD	77803	62821	71537	77804
5740	**ST**	P	*SW*	WD	77805	62822	71530	77806
5741	**ST**	P	*SW*	WD	77807	62823	71559	77808
5742	**ST**	P	*SW*	WD	77809	62824	71543	77810
5750	**ST**	P	*SW*	WD	77811	62825	71538	77812

Names (carried on TSO):

5711	SPIRIT OF RUGBY
5731	VARIETY CLUB
5735	The Royal Borough of Kingston
5750	Wimbledon Train Care

Class 455/8. First series. Pressure heating and ventilation.

DTSO. Lot No. 30972 York 1982–1984. –/74. 29.5 t.
MSO. Lot No. 30973 York 1982–1984. –/84. 45.6 t.
TSO. Lot No. 30974 York 1982–1984. –/84. 27.1 t.

Advertising Liveries: 5853 Cotes du Rhone wine (All over deep red with various images).
5856 Legoland Windsor (Yellow, blue and red with various images).
5868 Golden Jubilee/Hampton Court Palace (Gold with various images).
5869 New Royal British Legion poppy appeal (white with poppy images).

455801	**SN**	H	*SC*	SU	77579	62709	71637	77580
5802	**CX**	H	*SC*	SU	77581	62710	71664	77582
5803	**CX**	H	*SC*	SU	77583	62711	71639	77584
5804	**CX**	H	*SC*	SU	77585	62712	71640	77586
5805	**CX**	H	*SC*	SU	77587	62713	71641	77588
5806	**CX**	H	*SC*	SU	77589	62714	71642	77590
5807	**CX**	H	*SC*	SU	77591	62715	71643	77592
455808	**SN**	H	*SC*	SU	77593	62716	71644	77594
455809	**SN**	H	*SC*	SU	77595	62717	71645	77596
5810	**CX**	H	*SC*	SU	77597	62718	71646	77598
5811	**CX**	H	*SC*	SU	77599	62719	71647	77600
455812	**SN**	H	*SC*	SU	77601	62720	71648	77602
455813	**SN**	H	*SC*	SU	77603	62721	71649	77604
5814	**CX**	H	*SC*	SU	77605	62722	71650	77606
5815	**CX**	H	*SC*	SU	77607	62723	71651	77608
5816	**N**	H	*SC*	SU	77609	62724	71652	77633
5817	**N**	H	*SC*	SU	77611	62725	71653	77612
5818	**CX**	H	*SC*	SU	77613	62726	71654	77614
455819	**SN**	H	*SC*	SU	77615	62727	71655	77616
5820	**CX**	H	*SC*	SU	77617	62728	71656	77618
5821	**CX**	H	*SC*	SU	77619	62729	71657	77620
5822	**CX**	H	*SC*	SU	77621	62730	71658	77622
455823	**SN**	H	*SC*	SU	77623	62731	71659	77624
455824	**SN**	H	*SC*	SU	77637	62732	71660	77626
455825	**SN**	H	*SC*	SU	77627	62733	71661	77628
5826	**N**	H	*SC*	SU	77629	62734	71662	77630
5827	**CX**	H	*SC*	SU	77610	62735	71663	77632
5828	**N**	H	*SC*	SU	77631	62736	71638	77634
5829	**N**	H	*SC*	SU	77635	62737	71665	77636
5830	**N**	H	*SC*	SU	77625	62743	71666	77638
5831	**N**	H	*SC*	SU	77639	62739	71667	77640
5832	**U**	H	*SC*	SU	77641	62740	71668	77642
5833	**N**	H	*SC*	SU	77643	62741	71669	77644
5834	**N**	H	*SC*	SU	77645	62742	71670	77646
455835	**SN**	H	*SC*	SU	77647	62738	71671	77648
5836	**N**	H	*SC*	SU	77649	62744	71672	77650
5837	**N**	H	*SC*	SU	77651	62745	71673	77652
455838	**SN**	H	*SC*	SU	77653	62746	71674	77654
5839	**N**	H	*SC*	SU	77655	62747	71675	77656
5840	**N**	H	*SC*	SU	77657	62748	71676	77658

455841	**SN**	H	*SC*	SU	77659	62749	71677	77660
5842	**N**	H	*SC*	SU	77661	62750	71678	77662
5843	**N**	H	*SC*	SU	77663	62751	71679	77664
5844	**N**	H	*SC*	SU	77665	62752	71680	77666
5845	**N**	H	*SC*	SU	77667	62753	71681	77668
5846	**N**	H	*SC*	SU	77669	62754	71682	77670
5847	**ST**	P	*SW*	WD	77671	62755	71683	77672
5848	**ST**	P	*SW*	WD	77673	62756	71684	77674
5849	**ST**	P	*SW*	WD	77675	62757	71685	77676
5850	**ST**	P	*SW*	WD	77677	62758	71686	77678
5851	**ST**	P	*SW*	WD	77679	62759	71687	77680
5852	**ST**	P	*SW*	WD	77681	62760	71688	77682
5853	**AL**	P	*SW*	WD	77683	62761	71689	77684
5854	**ST**	P	*SW*	WD	77685	62762	71690	77686
5855	**ST**	P	*SW*	WD	77687	62763	71691	77688
5856	**AL**	P	*SW*	WD	77689	62764	71692	77690
5857	**ST**	P	*SW*	WD	77691	62765	71693	77692
5858	**ST**	P	*SW*	WD	77693	62766	71694	77694
5859	**ST**	P	*SW*	WD	77695	62767	71695	77696
5860	**ST**	P	*SW*	WD	77697	62768	71696	77698
5861	**ST**	P	*SW*	WD	77699	62769	71697	77700
5862	**ST**	P	*SW*	WD	77701	62770	71698	77702
5863	**N**	P	*SW*	WD	77703	62771	71699	77704
5864	**ST**	P	*SW*	WD	77705	62772	71700	77706
5865	**ST**	P	*SW*	WD	77707	62773	71701	77708
5866	**ST**	P	*SW*	WD	77709	62774	71702	77710
5867	**ST**	P	*SW*	WD	77711	62775	71703	77712
5868	**AL**	P	*SW*	WD	77713	62776	71704	77714
5869	**AL**	P	*SW*	WD	77715	62777	71705	77716
5870	**ST**	P	*SW*	WD	77717	62778	71706	77718
5871	**ST**	P	*SW*	WD	77719	62779	71707	77720
5872	**ST**	P	*SW*	WD	77721	62780	71708	77722
5873	**N**	P	*SW*	WD	77723	62781	71709	77724
5874	**ST**	P	*SW*	WD	77725	62782	71710	77726

Class 455/9. Third series. Convection heating.

DTSO. Lot No. 30991 York 1985. –/74. 29.5 t.
MSO. Lot No. 30992 York 1985. –/84. 45.6 t.
TSO. Lot No. 30993 York 1985. –/84. 27.1 t.
TSO. Lot No. 30932 Derby 1981. –/84. 27.1 t.

Note: † Prototype vehicle (67400) converted from a Class 210 DEMU.

Advertising Livery: 5904 South West Trains days out – "You really should get out more" (Blue and red with various images).

5901	**ST**	P	*SW*	WD	77813	62826	71714	77814
5902	**ST**	P	*SW*	WD	77815	62827	71715	77816
5903	**ST**	P	*SW*	WD	77817	62828	71716	77818
5904	**AL**	P	*SW*	WD	77819	62829	71717	77820
5905	**ST**	P	*SW*	WD	77821	62830	71725	77822
5906	**ST**	P	*SW*	WD	77823	62831	71719	77824

5907	**ST**	P	*SW*	WD	77825	62832	71720	77826
5908	**ST**	P	*SW*	WD	77827	62833	71721	77828
5909	**ST**	P	*SW*	WD	77829	62834	71722	77830
5910	**ST**	P	*SW*	WD	77831	62835	71723	77832
5911	**ST**	P	*SW*	WD	77833	62836	71724	77834
5912 †	**ST**	P	*SW*	WD	77835	62837	67400	77836
5913	**ST**	P	*SW*	WD	77837	62838	71726	77838
5914	**ST**	P	*SW*	WD	77839	62839	71727	77840
5915	**ST**	P	*SW*	WD	77841	62840	71728	77842
5916	**ST**	P	*SW*	WD	77843	62841	71729	77844
5917	**ST**	P	*SW*	WD	77845	62842	71730	77846
5918	**ST**	P	*SW*	WD	77847	62843	71732	77848
5919	**ST**	P	*SW*	WD	77849	62844	71718	77850
5920	**ST**	P	*SW*	WD	77851	62845	71733	77852
Spare	**ST**	P		ZG			71731	

CLASS 456   BREL YORK

South Central inner suburban units.

Formation: DMSO–DTSO.
Construction: Steel underframe, aluminium alloy body & roof.
Doors: Sliding.
Gangways: Within unit.   **Electrical Equipment:** 1966-type.
Traction Motors: Two GEC507-20J of 185 kW.
Bogies: P7 (motor) and T3 (trailer).   **Couplers:** Tightlock.
Maximum Speed: 75 m.p.h.   **Seating Layout:** 3+2 facing.
Dimensions: 20.18 x 2.82 m.   **Braking:** Disc brakes.
Heating & Ventilation: Convection.
Multiple Working: Within class and with Class 455.

DMSO. Lot No. 31073 1990–1991. –/79. 41.1 t.
DTSO. Lot No. 31074 1990–1991. –/73 1T. 31.4 t.

456 001	**N**	P	*SC*	SU	64735	78250
456 002	**N**	P	*SC*	SU	64736	78251
456 003	**N**	P	*SC*	SU	64737	78252
456 004	**N**	P	*SC*	SU	64738	78253
456 005	**N**	P	*SC*	SU	64739	78254
456 006	**N**	P	*SC*	SU	64740	78255
456 007	**N**	P	*SC*	SU	64741	78256
456 008	**N**	P	*SC*	SU	64742	78257
456 009	**N**	P	*SC*	SU	64743	78258
456 010	**N**	P	*SC*	SU	64744	78259
456 011	**N**	P	*SC*	SU	64745	78260
456 012	**N**	P	*SC*	SU	64746	78261
456 013	**N**	P	*SC*	SU	64747	78262
456 014	**N**	P	*SC*	SU	64748	78263
456 015	**N**	P	*SC*	SU	64749	78264
456 016	**N**	P	*SC*	SU	64750	78265
456 017	**N**	P	*SC*	SU	64751	78266
456 018	**N**	P	*SC*	SU	64752	78267

456 019	N	P	*SC*	SU	64753	78268
456 020	N	P	*SC*	SU	64754	78269
456 021	N	P	*SC*	SU	64755	78270
456 022	N	P	*SC*	SU	64756	78271
456 023	N	P	*SC*	SU	64757	78272
456 024	CX	P	*SC*	SU	64758	78273

Name (carried on DTSO): 456 024 Sir Cosmo Bonsor.

CLASS 458 JUNIPER ALSTOM BIRMINGHAM

South West Trains outer suburban units.
Formation: DMCO(A)–PTSO–MSO–DMCO(B).
SR designation: 4 Jop.

Construction: Steel.	**Doors:** Sliding plug.
Gangways: Throughout.	**Electrical Equipment:** IGBT control.

Traction Motors: Two Alstom ONIX 800 of 270 kW.

Couplers: Scharfenberg.	**Bogies:** ACR.
Maximum Speed: 100 m.p.h.	**Dimensions:** 21.01 x 2.82 m.

Seating Layout: 1: 2+2 facing, 2: 3+2 facing/unidirectional.
Braking: Disc and regenerative brakes. **Multiple Working:** Within class.
Heating & Ventilation: Air conditioning.

DMCO(A). Alstom Birmingham 1998–2000. 12/63. 45.2 t.
PTSO. Alstom Birmingham 1998–2000. –/49 1TD 2W. 33.3 t.
MSO. Alstom Birmingham 1998–2000. –/75 1T. 40.6 t.
DMCO(B). Alstom Birmingham 1998–2000. 12/63. 45.2 t.

8001	SW	P	*SW*	WD	67601	74001	74101	67701
8002	SW	P	*SW*	WD	67602	74002	74102	67702
8003	SW	P	*SW*	WD	67603	74003	74103	67703
8004	SW	P	*SW*	WD	67604	74004	74104	67704
8005	SW	P	*SW*	WD	67605	74005	74105	67705
8006	SW	P	*SW*	WD	67606	74006	74106	67706
8007	SW	P	*SW*	WD	67607	74007	74107	67707
8008	SW	P	*SW*	WD	67608	74008	74108	67708
8009	SW	P	*SW*	WD	67609	74009	74109	67709
8010	SW	P	*SW*	WD	67610	74010	74110	67710
8011	SW	P	*SW*	WD	67611	74011	74111	67711
8012	SW	P	*SW*	WD	67612	74012	74112	67712
8013	SW	P	*SW*	WD	67613	74013	74113	67713
8014	SW	P	*SW*	WD	67614	74014	74114	67714
8015	SW	P	*SW*	WD	67615	74015	74115	67715
8016	SW	P	*SW*	WD	67616	74016	74116	67716
8017	SW	P	*SW*	WD	67617	74017	74117	67717
8018	SW	P	*SW*	WD	67618	74018	74118	67718
8019	SW	P	*SW*	WD	67619	74019	74119	67719
8020	SW	P	*SW*	WD	67620	74020	74120	67720
8021	SW	P	*SW*	WD	67621	74021	74121	67721
8022	SW	P	*SW*	WD	67622	74022	74122	67722
8023	SW	P	*SW*	WD	67623	74023	74123	67723

8024	**SW**	P	*SW*	WD	67624	74024	74124	67724
8025	**SW**	P	*SW*	WD	67625	74025	74125	67725
8026	**SW**	P	*SW*	WD	67626	74026	74126	67726
8027	**SW**	P	*SW*	WD	67627	74027	74127	67727
8028	**SW**	P	*SW*	WD	67628	74028	74128	67728
8029	**SW**	P	*SW*	WD	67629	74029	74129	67729
8030	**SW**	P	*SW*	WD	67630	74030	74130	67730

CLASS 460   GEC-ALSTHOM JUNIPER

Gatwick Express units.

Formation: DMLFO–TFO–TCO–2MSO–TSO–MSO–DMSO.
SR designation: 8 Gat.
Construction: Steel.
Doors: Sliding plug.
Gangways: Within unit.
Electrical Equipment: IGBT control.
Traction Motors: Two Alstom ONIX 800 of 270 kW.
Couplers: Scharfenberg.
Bogies: ACR.
Maximum Speed: 100 m.p.h.
Seating Layout: 1: 2+1 facing, 2: 2+2 facing/unidirectional.
Dimensions: 21.01 m/19.9 m x 2.82 m. **Braking**: Disc and regenerative brakes.
Heating & Ventilation: Air conditioning. **Multiple Working**: Within class.

DMLFO. Alstom Birmingham 2000–2001. 10/– 42.6 t.
TFO. Alstom Birmingham 2000–2001. 28/– 1TD 1W. 33.5 t.
TCO. Alstom Birmingham 2000–2001. 9/42 1T. 34.9 t.
MSO(A). Alstom Birmingham 2000–2001. –/60. 42.5 t.
MSO(B). Alstom Birmingham 2000–2001. –/60. 42.5 t.
TSO. Alstom Birmingham 2000–2001. –/38 1TD 1W. 35.2 t.
MSO(C). Alstom Birmingham 2000–2001. –/60. 40.5 t.
DMSO. Alstom Birmingham 2000–2001. –/56. 45.3 t.

460001	**GV**	P	*GX*	SL	67901	74401	74411	74421
					74431	74441	74451	67911
460002	**GV**	P	*GX*	SL	67902	74402	74412	74422
					74432	74442	74452	67912
460003	**GV**	P	*GX*	SL	67903	74403	74413	74423
					74433	74443	74453	67913
460004	**GV**	P	*GX*	SL	67904	74404	74414	74424
					74434	74444	74454	67914
460005	**GV**	P	*GX*	SL	67905	74405	74415	74425
					74435	74445	74455	67915
460006	**GV**	P	*GX*	SL	67906	74406	74416	74426
					74436	74446	74456	67916
460007	**GV**	P	*GX*	SL	67907	74407	74417	74427
					74437	74447	74457	67917
460008	**GV**	P	*GX*	SL	67908	74408	74418	74428
					74438	74448	74458	67918

CLASS 465   NETWORKER

Formation: DMSO–TSO–TSO–DMSO.
Construction: Welded aluminium alloy.
Doors: Sliding plug.
Gangways: Within unit.   **Electrical Equipment**: GTO inverters.
Traction Motors: Four Brush TIM970 (Classes 465/0 and 465/1) or GEC-Alsthom G352AY (Class 465/2) three-phase induction motors of 280 kW.
Couplers: Tightlock.
Bogies: BREL P3/T3 (Classes 465/0 and 465/1) SRP BP62/BT52 (Class 465/2).
Maximum Speed: 75 m.p.h.   **Dimensions**: 20.89/20.16 x 2.82 m.
Seating Layout: 3+2 (* 2+2) facing/unidirectional.
Braking: Disc, rheostatic and regenerative.
Multiple Working: Within class and with Classes 365 and 466.

64759–64808. DMSO(A). Lot No. 31100 BREL York 1991–1993. –/86 (* –/74). 38.9 t.
64809–64858. DMSO(B). Lot No. 31100 BREL York 1991–1993. –/86 (* –/74). 39 t.
65700–65749. DMSO(A). Lot No. 31103 Metro-Cammell 1991–1993. –/86. 38.8 t.
65750–65799. DMSO(B). Lot No. 31103 Metro-Cammell 1991–1993. –/86. 38.9 t.
65800–65846. DMSO(A). Lot No. 31130 ABB York 1993–1994. –/86. 38.9 t.
65847–65893. DMSO(B). Lot No. 31130 ABB York 1993–1994. –/86. 39 t.
72028–72126 (even nos.). TSO. Lot No. 31102 BREL York 1991–93. –/90 (* –/80). 29.5 t.
72029–72127 (odd nos.). TSO. Lot No. 31101 BREL York 1991–93. –/86 1T (* –/76 1T). 28.6 t.
72719–72817 (odd nos.). TSO. Lot No. 31104 Metro-Cammell 1991–1992. –/86 1T. 30.2 t.
72720–72818 (even nos.). TSO. Lot No. 31105 Metro-Cammell 1991–1992. –/90. 29.1 t.
72900–72992 (even nos.). TSO. Lot No. 31102 ABB York 1993–1994. –/90. 29.5 t.
72901–72993 (odd nos.). TSO. Lot No. 31101 ABB York 1993–1994. –/86 1T. 28.6 t.

Class 465/0. Built by BREL/ABB.

465 001		**CB**	H	*SE*	SG	64759	72028	72029	64809
465 002		**CB**	H	*SE*	SG	64760	72030	72031	64810
465 003		**CB**	H	*SE*	SG	64761	72032	72033	64811
465 004		**NT**	H	*SE*	SG	64762	72034	72035	64812
465 005		**NT**	H	*SE*	SG	64763	72036	72037	64813
465 006		**CB**	H	*SE*	SG	64764	72038	72039	64814
465 007		**CB**	H	*SE*	SG	64765	72040	72041	64815
465 008		**CB**	H	*SE*	SG	64766	72042	72043	64816
465 009		**CB**	H	*SE*	SG	64767	72044	72045	64817
465 010		**CB**	H	*SE*	SG	64768	72046	72047	64818
465 011		**CB**	H	*SE*	SG	64769	72048	72049	64819
465 012		**CB**	H	*SE*	SG	64770	72050	72051	64820
465 013		**CB**	H	*SE*	SG	64771	72052	72053	64821
465 014	*	**CB**	H	*SE*	SG	64772	72054	72055	64822
465 015		**CB**	H	*SE*	SG	64773	72056	72057	64823
465 016		**CB**	H	*SE*	SG	64774	72058	72059	64824
465 017		**CB**	H	*SE*	SG	64775	72060	72061	64825
465 018		**CB**	H	*SE*	SG	64776	72062	72063	64826
465 019		**CB**	H	*SE*	SG	64777	72064	72065	64827
465 020		**CB**	H	*SE*	SG	64778	72066	72067	64828
465 021		**NT**	H	*SE*	SG	64779	72068	72069	64829

465 022	**NT**	H	*SE*	SG	64780	72070	72071	64830
465 023	**NT**	H	*SE*	SG	64781	72072	72073	64831
465 024	**NT**	H	*SE*	SG	64782	72074	72075	64832
465 025	**NT**	H	*SE*	SG	64783	72076	72077	64833
465 026	**NT**	H	*SE*	SG	64784	72078	72079	64834
465 027	**NT**	H	*SE*	SG	64785	72080	72081	64835
465 028	**NT**	H	*SE*	SG	64786	72082	72083	64836
465 029	**NT**	H	*SE*	SG	64787	72084	72085	64837
465 030	**NT**	H	*SE*	SG	64788	72086	72087	64838
465 031	**NT**	H	*SE*	SG	64789	72088	72089	64839
465 032	**NT**	H	*SE*	SG	64790	72090	72091	64840
465 033	**NT**	H	*SE*	SG	64791	72092	72093	64841
465 034	**NT**	H	*SE*	SG	64792	72094	72095	64842
465 035	**NT**	H	*SE*	SG	64793	72096	72097	64843
465 036	**NT**	H	*SE*	SG	64794	72098	72099	64844
465 037	**NT**	H	*SE*	SG	64795	72100	72101	64845
465 038	**NT**	H	*SE*	SG	64796	72102	72103	64846
465 039	**NT**	H	*SE*	SG	64797	72104	72105	64847
465 040	**NT**	H	*SE*	SG	64798	72106	72107	64848
465 041	**NT**	H	*SE*	SG	64799	72108	72109	64849
465 042	**NT**	H	*SE*	SG	64800	72110	72111	64850
465 043	**NT**	H	*SE*	SG	64801	72112	72113	64851
465 044	**NT**	H	*SE*	SG	64802	72114	72115	64852
465 045	**NT**	H	*SE*	SG	64803	72116	72117	64853
465 046	**NT**	H	*SE*	SG	64804	72118	72119	64854
465 047	**NT**	H	*SE*	SG	64805	72120	72121	64855
465 048	**NT**	H	*SE*	SG	64806	72122	72123	64856
465 049	**NT**	H	*SE*	SG	64807	72124	72125	64857
465 050	**NT**	H	*SE*	SG	64808	72126	72127	64858

Class 465/1. Built by BREL/ABB. Similar to Class 465/0 but with detail differences.

465 151	**NT**	H	*SE*	SG	65800	72900	72901	65847
465 152	**NT**	H	*SE*	SG	65801	72902	72903	65848
465 153	**NT**	H	*SE*	SG	65802	72904	72905	65849
465 154	**NT**	H	*SE*	SG	65803	72906	72907	65850
465 155	**NT**	H	*SE*	SG	65804	72908	72909	65851
465 156	**NT**	H	*SE*	SG	65805	72910	72911	65852
465 157	**NT**	H	*SE*	SG	65806	72912	72913	65853
465 158	**NT**	H	*SE*	SG	65807	72914	72915	65854
465 159	**NT**	H	*SE*	SG	65808	72916	72917	65855
465 160	**NT**	H	*SE*	SG	65809	72918	72919	65856
465 161	**NT**	H	*SE*	SG	65810	72920	72921	65857
465 162	**NT**	H	*SE*	SG	65811	72922	72923	65858
465 163	**NT**	H	*SE*	SG	65812	72924	72925	65859
465 164	**NT**	H	*SE*	SG	65813	72926	72927	65860
465 165	**NT**	H	*SE*	SG	65814	72928	72929	65861
465 166	**NT**	H	*SE*	SG	65815	72930	72931	65862
465 167	**NT**	H	*SE*	SG	65816	72932	72933	65863
465 168	**NT**	H	*SE*	SG	65817	72934	72935	65864
465 169	**NT**	H	*SE*	SG	65818	72936	72937	65865

465 170	**NT**	H	*SE*	SG	65819	72938	72939	65866
465 171	**NT**	H	*SE*	SG	65820	72940	72941	65867
465 172	**NT**	H	*SE*	SG	65821	72942	72943	65868
465 173	**NT**	H	*SE*	SG	65822	72944	72945	65869
465 174	**NT**	H	*SE*	SG	65823	72946	72947	65870
465 175	**NT**	H	*SE*	SG	65824	72948	72949	65871
465 176	**NT**	H	*SE*	SG	65825	72950	72951	65872
465 177	**NT**	H	*SE*	SG	65826	72952	72953	65873
465 178	**NT**	H	*SE*	SG	65827	72954	72955	65874
465 179	**NT**	H	*SE*	SG	65828	72956	72957	65875
465 180	**NT**	H	*SE*	SG	65829	72958	72959	65876
465 181	**NT**	H	*SE*	SG	65830	72960	72961	65877
465 182	**NT**	H	*SE*	SG	65831	72962	72963	65878
465 183	**NT**	H	*SE*	SG	65832	72964	72965	65879
465 184	**NT**	H	*SE*	SG	65833	72966	72967	65880
465 185	**NT**	H	*SE*	SG	65834	72968	72969	65881
465 186	**NT**	H	*SE*	SG	65835	72970	72971	65882
465 187	**NT**	H	*SE*	SG	65836	72972	72973	65883
465 188	**NT**	H	*SE*	SG	65837	72974	72975	65884
465 189	**NT**	H	*SE*	SG	65838	72976	72977	65885
465 190	**NT**	H	*SE*	SG	65839	72978	72979	65886
465 191	**NT**	H	*SE*	SG	65840	72980	72981	65887
465 192	**NT**	H	*SE*	SG	65841	72982	72983	65888
465 193	**NT**	H	*SE*	SG	65842	72984	72985	65889
465 194	**NT**	H	*SE*	SG	65843	72986	72987	65890
465 195	**NT**	H	*SE*	SG	65844	72988	72989	65891
465 196	**NT**	H	*SE*	SG	65845	72990	72991	65892
465 197	**NT**	H	*SE*	SG	65846	72992	72993	65893

Class 465/2. Built by Metro-Cammell.

465 201	**NT**	A	*SE*	SG	65700	72719	72720	65750
465 202	**CN**	A	*SE*	SG	65701	72721	72722	65751
465 203	**NT**	A	*SE*	SG	65702	72723	72724	65752
465 204	**NT**	A	*SE*	SG	65703	72725	72726	65753
465 205	**NT**	A	*SE*	SG	65704	72727	72728	65754
465 206	**CN**	A	*SE*	SG	65705	72729	72730	65755
465 207	**CN**	A	*SE*	SG	65706	72731	72732	65756
465 208	**NT**	A	*SE*	SG	65707	72733	72734	65757
465 209	**NT**	A	*SE*	SG	65708	72735	72736	65758
465 210	**CN**	A	*SE*	SG	65709	72737	72738	65759
465 211	**NT**	A	*SE*	SG	65710	72739	72740	65760
465 212	**NT**	A	*SE*	SG	65711	72741	72742	65761
465 213	**CN**	A	*SE*	SG	65712	72743	72744	65762
465 214	**NT**	A	*SE*	SG	65713	72745	72746	65763
465 215	**NT**	A	*SE*	SG	65714	72747	72748	65764
465 216	**CN**	A	*SE*	SG	65715	72749	72750	65765
465 217	**NT**	A	*SE*	SG	65716	72751	72752	65766
465 218	**NT**	A	*SE*	SG	65717	72753	72754	65767
465 219	**NT**	A	*SE*	SG	65718	72755	72756	65768
465 220	**CN**	A	*SE*	SG	65719	72757	72758	65769
465 221	**NT**	A	*SE*	SG	65720	72759	72760	65770

465 222	**CN**	A	*SE*	SG	65721	72761	72762	65771
465 223	**CN**	A	*SE*	SG	65722	72763	72764	65772
465 224	**CN**	A	*SE*	SG	65723	72765	72766	65773
465 225	**NT**	A	*SE*	SG	65724	72767	72768	65774
465 226	**NT**	A	*SE*	SG	65725	72769	72770	65775
465 227	**NT**	A	*SE*	SG	65726	72771	72772	65776
465 228	**NT**	A	*SE*	SG	65727	72773	72774	65777
465 229	**CN**	A	*SE*	SG	65728	72775	72776	65778
465 230	**NT**	A	*SE*	SG	65729	72777	72778	65779
465 231	**CN**	A	*SE*	SG	65730	72779	72780	65780
465 232	**NT**	A	*SE*	SG	65731	72781	72782	65781
465 233	**CN**	A	*SE*	SG	65732	72783	72784	65782
465 234	**NT**	A	*SE*	SG	65733	72785	72786	65783
465 235	**NT**	A	*SE*	SG	65734	72787	72788	65784
465 236	**NT**	A	*SE*	SG	65735	72789	72790	65785
465 237	**CN**	A	*SE*	SG	65736	72791	72792	65786
465 238	**NT**	A	*SE*	SG	65737	72793	72794	65787
465 239	**NT**	A	*SE*	SG	65738	72795	72796	65788
465 240	**CN**	A	*SE*	SG	65739	72797	72798	65789
465 241	**CN**	A	*SE*	SG	65740	72799	72800	65790
465 242	**CN**	A	*SE*	SG	65741	72801	72802	65791
465 243	**CN**	A	*SE*	SG	65742	72803	72804	65792
465 244	**NT**	A	*SE*	SG	65743	72805	72806	65793
465 245	**NT**	A	*SE*	SG	65744	72807	72808	65794
465 246	**CN**	A	*SE*	SG	65745	72809	72810	65795
465 247	**CN**	A	*SE*	SG	65746	72811	72812	65796
465 248	**NT**	A	*SE*	SG	65747	72813	72814	65797
465 249	**NT**	A	*SE*	SG	65748	72815	72816	65798
465 250	**NT**	A	*SE*	SG	65749	72817	72818	65799

CLASS 466   NETWORKER   GEC-ALSTHOM

Formation: DMSO–DTSO.
Construction: Welded aluminium alloy.
Doors: Sliding plug.
Gangways: Within unit.   **Electrical Equipment:** GTO inverters.
Traction Motors: Four GEC-Alsthom G352AY three-phase induction motors of 280 kW.
Couplers: Tightlock.   **Bogies:** SRP BP62/BT52.
Maximum Speed: 75 m.p.h.   **Dimensions:** 20.89 x 2.82 m.
Seating Layout: 3+2 (* 2+2) facing/unidirectional.
Braking: Disc, rheostatic and regenerative.
Multiple Working: Within class and Classes 365 and 465.

DMSO. Lot No. 31128 Birmingham 1993–1994. –/86 (* –/72). 38.8 t.
DTSO. Lot No. 31129 Birmingham 1993–1994. –/82 1T (* –/68 1T). 33.2 t.

466 001	**NT**	A	*SE*	SG	64860	78312
466 002	**CN**	A	*SE*	SG	64861	78313
466 003	**CN**	A	*SE*	SG	64862	78314
466 004	**CN**	A	*SE*	SG	64863	78315
466 005	**CN**	A	*SE*	SG	64864	78316

466 006	**CN**	A	*SE*	SG	64865	78317
466 007	**CN**	A	*SE*	SG	64866	78318
466 008	**NT**	A	*SE*	SG	64867	78319
466 009	**NT**	A	*SE*	SG	64868	78320
466 010	**NT**	A	*SE*	SG	64869	78321
466 011	**NT**	A	*SE*	SG	64870	78322
466 012	**NT**	A	*SE*	SG	64871	78323
466 013	**NT**	A	*SE*	SG	64872	78324
466 014	**NT**	A	*SE*	SG	64873	78325
466 015	**NT**	A	*SE*	SG	64874	78326
466 016	**NT**	A	*SE*	SG	64875	78327
466 017 *	**NT**	A	*SE*	SG	64876	78328
466 018	**CN**	A	*SE*	SG	64877	78329
466 019	**NT**	A	*SE*	SG	64878	78330
466 020	**CN**	A	*SE*	SG	64879	78331
466 021	**CN**	A	*SE*	SG	64880	78332
466 022	**CN**	A	*SE*	SG	64881	78333
466 023	**CN**	A	*SE*	SG	64882	78334
466 024	**CN**	A	*SE*	SG	64883	78335
466 025	**CN**	A	*SE*	SG	64884	78336
466 026	**NT**	A	*SE*	SG	64885	78337
466 027	**NT**	A	*SE*	SG	64886	78338
466 028	**NT**	A	*SE*	SG	64887	78339
466 029	**NT**	A	*SE*	SG	64888	78340
466 030	**NT**	A	*SE*	SG	64889	78341
466 031	**NT**	A	*SE*	SG	64890	78342
466 032	**CN**	A	*SE*	SG	64891	78343
466 033	**CN**	A	*SE*	SG	64892	78344
466 034	**CN**	A	*SE*	SG	64893	78345
466 035	**CN**	A	*SE*	SG	64894	78346
466 036	**NT**	A	*SE*	SG	64895	78347
466 037	**CN**	A	*SE*	SG	64896	78348
466 038	**NT**	A	*SE*	SG	64897	78349
466 039	**NT**	A	*SE*	SG	64898	78350
466 040	**NT**	A	*SE*	SG	64899	78351
466 041	**NT**	A	*SE*	SG	64900	78352
466 042	**NT**	A	*SE*	SG	64901	78353
466 043	**NT**	A	*SE*	SG	64902	78354

CLASS 483   METRO-CAMMELL

Built 1938 onwards for LTE. Converted 1989–1990 for Isle of Wight Line.

Formation: DMSO(A)–DMSO(B).
System: 660 V DC third rail.
Construction: Steel.   **Doors**: Sliding.
Gangways: None. End doors.   **Electrical Equipment**: IGBT control.
Traction Motors: Two Crompton Parkinson/GEC/BTH LT100 of 125 kW.
Couplers: Wedglock.   **Bogies**: LT design.
Maximum Speed: 45 m.p.h.   **Multiple Working**: Within class.
Seating Layout: Longitudinal or 2+2 facing/unidirectional.
Dimensions: 16.00 x 2.69 m.   **Braking**: Tread brakes.

Notes: The last three numbers of the unit number only are carried.
Former London Underground numbers are shown in parentheses.

DMSO (A). Lot No. 31071. –/40. 27.5 t.
DMSO (B). Lot No. 31072. –/42. 27.5 t.

Non-standard livery: 483 007 Original London Transport Maroon and cream.

483 002	**IL**	H	*IL*	RY	122	(10221)	225 (11142)
483 003	**N**	H		RY	123	(10116)	221 (11184)
483 004	**IL**	H	*IL*	RY	124	(10205)	224 (11205)
483 006	**IL**	H	*IL*	RY	126	(10297)	226 (11297)
483 007	**0**	H	*IL*	RY	127	(10291)	227 (11291)
483 008	**IL**	H	*IL*	RY	128	(10255)	228 (11255)
483 009	**IL**	H	*IL*	RY	129	(10289)	229 (11229)

CLASS 488   BR DERBY

Converted 1983–1984 from Mk. 2F FOs and TSOs for Victoria–Gatwick services.
The seating layout was modified with and the removal of one toilet to provide
additional luggage space. Two sets were still in use as this book closed for press,
covering for non-available Class 460s.
Formation: TFOH–TSO (Class 488/3 only)–TSOH.
Construction: Steel.   **Doors**: Slam.
Gangways: Throughout.   **Couplers**: Buckeye.
Bogies: B4.   **Maximum Speed**: 90 m.p.h.
Seating Layout: 1: 2+1 facing 2: 2+2 facing.
Dimensions: 20.18 x 2.82 m.   **Braking**: Tread brakes.
Heating & Ventilation: Air conditioning.
Multiple Working: SR.

72500–72509. TFOH. Lot No. 30859 Derby 1973–1974. 41/– 1T. 35 t.
72602–72614/72616–72618/72620–72644/72646/72647. TSOH. Lot No. 30860
Derby 1973–1974. –/48 1T. 35 t.
72615/72619/72645. TSOH. Lot No. 30846 Derby 1973. –/48 1T. 35 t.
72701–72718. TSO. Lot No. 30860 Derby 1973–1974. –/48 1T. 35 t.

Notes: Sets 8307 and 8309 are used as part of Network Rail's Radio Survey
Train. Set 8316 is used in the Network Rail Ultrasonic Test Train.

Advertising Livery: As **GX** but with a deep blue instead of a white lower bodyside, advertising Continental Airlines.

CLASS 488/2. TFOH–TSOH. **Note:** TFOH fitted with public telephone.

8201	**GX**	GB		PY	72500 (3413)	72638 (6068)
8202	**GX**	P	*GX*	SL	72501 (3382)	72617 (6086)
8206	**GX**	P	*GX*	SL	72505 (3415)	72629 (6048)
8207	**AL**	P		PY	72506 (3335)	72642 (6076)
8208	**AL**	GB		NC	72507 (3412)	72643 (6040)
8209	**GX**	P	*GX*	SL	72508 (3409)	72644 (6039)
8210	**AL**	P		PY	72509 (3398)	72635 (6128)
Spare	**AL**	P		PY	72502 (3321)	
Spare	**AL**	NR		ZA		72640 (6097)
Spare	**AL**	NR		ZA		72641 (6079)

CLASS 488/3. TSOH–(TSO)–TSOH.

8303	**GX**	NR		ZA	72603 (6093)	72702 (6099)	72608 (6077)
8304	**AL**	P		PY	72606 (6084)	72703 (6075)	72611 (6083)
8306	**GX**	P		PY	72607 (6020)	72705 (6032)	72610 (6074)
8307	**RK**	NR	*SO*	ZA	72612 (6156)	72706 (6143)	72613 (6126)
8308	**RK**	NR	*SO*	ZA	72614 (6090)	72707 (6127)	72615 (5938)
8309	**RK**	NR	*SO*	ZA	72616 (6007)	72708 (6095)	72639 (6070)
8310	**AL**	P		PY	72618 (6044)	72709 (5982)	72619 (5909)
8311	**GX**	P	*GX*	SL	72620 (6140)	72710 (6003)	72621 (6108)
8312	**GX**	GB		NC	72622 (6004)	72711 (6109)	72623 (6118)
8313	**GX**	P	*GX*	SL	72624 (5972)	72712 (6091)	72625 (6085)
8315	**GX**	GB		NC	72636 (6071)	72714 (6092)	72645 (5942)
8316	**RK**	NR	*SO*	ZA	72630 (6094)		72631 (6096)
Spare	**AL**	CD		MM		72713 (6023)	

CLASS 489   BR EASTLEIGH

Converted 1983–1984 from Class 414/3 (2 Hap) DMBSOs to work with Class 488.

Formation: DMLV.
Construction: Steel.   **Doors:** Slam.
Gangways: Gangwayed at inner end only. **Electrical Equipment:** 1966-type.
Traction Motors: Two EE507 of 185 kW. **Couplers:** Buckeye.
Bogies: Mark 4.   **Maximum Speed:** 90 m.p.h.
Dimensions: 20.45 x 2.82 m.   **Braking:** Tread brakes.
Multiple Working: SR.

DMLV. Lot No. 30452 1959. 40.5 t.

9101	**GX**	P		PY	68500 (61269)
9102	**GX**	NR		ZA	68501 (61281)
9104	**GX**	P	*GX*	SL	68503 (61277)
9105	**GX**	GB		NC	68504 (61286)
9106	**GX**	GB		NC	68505 (61299)
9108	**GX**	P	*GX*	SL	68507 (61267)
9109	**GX**	NR		ZA	68508 (61272)
9110	**GX**	P	*GX*	SL	68509 (61280)

▲ South Central units 377 105 and 377 106 depart Littlehampton on a test run from Horsham to Brighton Lovers Walk depot on 22/04/03.   **Chris Wilson**

▼ Virgin West Coast "Pendolino" 390 022 is seen near Stableford with the 17.15 London Euston–Manchester Piccadilly on 20/06/03.   **Hugh Ballantyne**

▲ Stagecoach-liveried Class 412 2315 is seen at Millbrook (Hants.) forming the 11.06 Poole–London Waterloo on 12/09/03. This is one of seven Class 412 former "4 Beps" converted to Ceps by replacement of their buffet cars with TSOs.
Kim Fullbrook

▼ Carrying the attractive South Central livery, Class 421 1861 is seen at Goring-by-Sea on the 11.44 Littlehampton–London Victoria on 09/04/02.   **Brian Denton**

▲ Class 423/1 3571 approaches Otford Junction with the 13.42 Canterbury West–London Victoria on 25/04/03. Connex lost the South Eastern franchise in November 2003, although it is likely that this and other variants of Connex livery will still be around for some time.　　**Ian G. Feather**

▼ South West Trains-liveried 2419 arrives at Hamworthy with the 09.30 London Waterloo–Weymouth on 28/09/01.　　**Hugh Ballantyne**

▲ On 13/10/03, the first day of service for South West Trains Class 450 "Desiro" units on this route, 450 026 brings up the rear of the 12.47 Basingstoke–London Waterloo at Surbiton, led by 450 015. **Alan Yearsley**

▼ South Central-liveried 455 823 departs Redhill on the 09.03 (SuO) to London Bridge on 15/06/03. **Alex Dasi-Sutton**

▲ 456 023 arrives at Wandsworth Road with the 16.10 London Victoria–London Bridge via Peckham Rye on 29/07/02. Like all except one of the class, this unit is still in Network SouthEast livery. **Chris Booth**

▼ South West Trains-liveried Class 458 8016 is seen nearing its destination with the 10.26 London Waterloo–Guildford on 03/07/01. **Chris Wilson**

▲ On 17/10/02 Gatwick Express-liveried 460 004 passes Horley on a London Victoria-bound service. **Rodney Lissenden**

▼ Looking superb in Connex's black and white livery, 465 237 arrives at Otford with a Sevenoaks–London Blackfriars service on 18/03/03. **Rodney Lissenden**

▲ Lovingly restored to its original London Transport red livery (save for the mandatory yellow warning panels), Island Line unit 483 007 was caught on camera at Sandown with the 16.08 Ryde Pier Head–Shanklin on 09/07/03. In the background a "Dinosaur"-liveried unit can be seen bound for Ryde Pier Head. **Martyn Hilbert**

▼ GNER-liveried Eurostar set 3303/04 passes Black Carr, Doncaster with the 12.05 "White Rose" Leeds–London King's Cross service on 13/09/03. **Gavin Morrison**

▲ On 18/08/03, 507 031, in old MerseyRail livery, departs Chester with the 16.45 to Liverpool Central. Note the Class 175 DMU maintenance depot in the background. **Robert Pritchard**

▼ 508 303 departs from London Euston on the 12.17 "Silverlink Metro" service to Watford Junction on 28/06/03. This is one of three ex-Merseyrail Class 508s transferred to Silverlink for exclusive use on these services. **Bob Sweet**

CLASS 507   BREL YORK

Formation: BDMSO–TSO–DMSO.
System: 750 V DC third rail.
Traction Motors: Four GEC G310AZ of 82.125 kW.
Construction: Steel underframe, aluminium alloy body and roof.
Doors: Sliding.
Gangways: Within unit + end doors.   **Bogies:** BX1.
Couplers: Tightlock   **Maximum Speed:** 75 m.p.h.
Seating Layout: 3+2 facing.   **Dimensions:** 20.18 x 2.82 m.
Braking: Disc and rheostatic.
Multiple Working: Within class and with Class 508.

BDMSO. Lot No. 30906 1978–1980. –/68 1W. 37.06 t.
TSO. Lot No. 30907 1978–1980. –/86. 25.60 t.
DMSO. Lot No. 30908 1978–1980. –/68 1W. 35.62 t.

507 001	MT	A	*ME*	BD	64367	71342	64405
507 002	MT	A	*ME*	BD	64368	71343	64406
507 003	MY	A	*ME*	BD	64369	71344	64407
507 004	MY	A	*ME*	BD	64388	71345	64408
507 005	MY	A	*ME*	BD	64371	71346	64409
507 006	MY	A	*ME*	BD	64372	71347	64410
507 007	MT	A	*ME*	BD	64373	71348	64411
507 008	MY	A	*ME*	BD	64374	71349	64412
507 009	MY	A	*ME*	BD	64375	71350	64413
507 010	MT	A	*ME*	BD	64376	71351	64414
507 011	MT	A	*ME*	BD	64377	71352	64415
507 012	MT	A	*ME*	BD	64378	71353	64416
507 013	MY	A	*ME*	BD	64379	71354	64417
507 014	MT	A	*ME*	BD	64380	71355	64418
507 015	MT	A	*ME*	BD	64381	71356	64419
507 016	MT	A	*ME*	BD	64382	71357	64420
507 017	MT	A	*ME*	BD	64383	71358	64421
507 018	MT	A	*ME*	BD	64384	71359	64422
507 019	MT	A	*ME*	BD	64385	71360	64423
507 020	MT	A	*ME*	BD	64386	71361	64424
507 021	MY	A	*ME*	BD	64387	71362	64425
507 023	MT	A	*ME*	BD	64389	71364	64427
507 024	MY	A	*ME*	BD	64390	71365	64428
507 025	MY	A	*ME*	BD	64391	71366	64429
507 026	MY	A	*ME*	BD	64392	71367	64430
507 027	MT	A	*ME*	BD	64393	71368	64431
507 028	MT	A	*ME*	BD	64394	71369	64432
507 029	MT	A	*ME*	BD	64395	71370	64433
507 030	MT	A	*ME*	BD	64396	71371	64434
507 031	MT	A	*ME*	BD	64397	71372	64435
507 032	MY	A	*ME*	BD	64398	71373	64436
507 033	MT	A	*ME*	BD	64399	71374	64437

CLASS 508   BREL YORK

Formation: DMSO–TSO–BDMSO.
System: 750 V DC third rail.
Traction Motors: Four GEC G310AZ of 82.125 kW.
Construction: Steel underframe, aluminium alloy body and roof.
Doors: Sliding.
Gangways: Within unit + end doors.   **Bogies:** BX1.
Couplers: Tightlock   **Maximum Speed:** 75 m.p.h.
Seating Layout: 3+2 facing.   **Dimensions:** 20.18 x 2.82 m.
Braking: Disc and rheostatic.
Multiple Working: Within class and with Class 507.

DMSO. Lot No. 30979 1979–1980. –/68 (* –/56) 1W. 36.2 t.
TSO. Lot No. 30980 1979–1980. –/86 (* –/72). 26.7 t.
BDMSO. Lot No. 30981 1979–1980. –/68 (* –/56) 1W. 36.6 t.

Class 508/1. Standard design.

Notes: Units currently shown as stored out of use at Alstom, Eastleigh (ZG) are
being refurbished for Merseyrail.
Refurbished Merseyrail units (shown as *) have 2+2 high-back seating.

508 103		**MT**	A	*ME*	BD	64651	71485	64694
508 104		**MT**	A	*ME*	BD	64652	71486	64695
508 108	*	**ME**	A	*ME*	BD	64656	71490	64699
508 110	*	**ME**	A	*ME*	BD	64658	71492	64701
508 111		**MY**	A	*ME*	BD	64659	71493	64702
508 112		**MT**	A	*ME*	BD	64660	71494	64703
508 114		**MT**	A	*ME*	BD	64662	71496	64705
508 115		**MY**	A	*ME*	BD	64663	71497	64706
508 117		**MY**	A	*ME*	BD	64665	71499	64708
508 120		**MT**	A		ZG	64668	71502	64711
508 122		**MT**	A		ZG	64670	71504	64713
508 123		**MT**	A		ZG	64671	71505	64714
508 124		**MT**	A	*ME*	BD	64672	71506	64715
508 125		**MT**	A	*ME*	BD	64673	71507	64716
508 126		**MT**	A	*ME*	BD	64674	71508	64717
508 127		**MY**	A	*ME*	BD	64675	71509	64718
508 128		**MY**	A	*ME*	BD	64676	71510	64719
508 130		**MT**	A	*ME*	BD	64678	71512	64721
508 131	*	**ME**	A	*ME*	BD	64679	71513	64722
508 134		**MT**	A	*ME*	BD	64682	71516	64725
508 136		**MT**	A	*ME*	BD	64684	71518	64727
508 137		**MT**	A	*ME*	BD	64685	71519	64728
508 138		**MY**	A	*ME*	BD	64686	71520	64729
508 139		**MT**	A	*ME*	BD	64687	71521	64730
508 140		**MT**	A	*ME*	BD	64688	71522	64731
508 141		**MT**	A	*ME*	BD	64689	71523	64732
508 143		**MT**	A	*ME*	BD	64691	71525	64734

Class 508/2. Facelifted South Eastern Trains units. Refurbished 1998–1999 by Wessex Traincare/Alstom, Eastleigh.

DMSO. Lot No. 30979 1979–1980. –/66. 36.2 t.
TSO. Lot No. 30980 1979–1980. –/79. 26.7 t.
BDMSO. Lot No. 30981 1979–1980. –/74. 36.6 t.

508 201	(508 101)	**CX**	A	*SE*	GI	64649	71483	64692
508 202	(508 105)	**CX**	A	*SE*	GI	64653	71487	64696
508 203	(508 106)	**CX**	A	*SE*	GI	64654	71488	64697
508 204	(508 107)	**CX**	A	*SE*	GI	64655	71489	64698
508 205	(508 109)	**CX**	A	*SE*	GI	64657	71491	64700
508 206	(508 113)	**CX**	A	*SE*	GI	64661	71495	64704
508 207	(508 116)	**CX**	A	*SE*	GI	64664	71498	64707
508 208	(508 119)	**CX**	A	*SE*	GI	64667	71501	64710
508 209	(508 121)	**CX**	A	*SE*	GI	64669	71503	64712
508 210	(508 129)	**CX**	A	*SE*	GI	64677	71511	64720
508 211	(508 132)	**CX**	A	*SE*	GI	64680	71514	64723
508 212	(508 133)	**CX**	A	*SE*	GI	64681	71515	64724

Class 508/3. Facelifted units for Silverlink for use on Euston–Watford Junction services. Refurbished 2002–2003 by Alstom, Eastleigh. Details as Class 508/1.

508 301	(508 102)	**SL**	A	*SL*	WN	64650	71484	64693
508 302	(508 135)	**SL**	A	*SL*	WN	64683	71517	64726
508 303	(508 142)	**SL**	A	*SL*	WN	64690	71524	64733

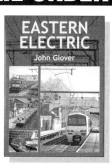

3. EUROSTAR UNITS (CLASS 373)

Eurostar units were built for and are normally used on services between Britain and Continental Europe via the Channel Tunnel. Apart from such workings units may be used as follows:

• SNCF-owned units 3203/3204/3225/3226/3227/3228 have been removed from the Eurostar pool, and are in a pool which normally only operate SNCF-internal services between Paris and Lille.

• Certain 8-car sets are used on a daily basis by GNER for its "White Rose" services.

Each train consists of two Eurostar units coupled, with a motor car at each driving end. Services starting from/terminating at London Waterloo International are formed of two 10-car units coupled, whilst those to/from other British destinations (yet to commence) will be formed of two 8-car units coupled. All units are articulated with an extra motor bogie on the coach adjacent to the motor car.

DM–MSO–4TSO–RB–2TFO–TBFO or DM–MSO–3TSO–RB–TFO–TBFO. Gangwayed within pair of units. Air conditioned.
Construction: Steel.
Supply Systems: 25 kV AC 50 Hz overhead or 3000 V DC overhead or 750 V DC third rail (* also equipped for 1500 V DC overhead operation).
Wheel Arrangement: Bo–Bo + Bo–2–2–2–2–2–2–2–2.
Length: 22.15 m (DM), 21.85 m (MS & TBF), 18.70 m (other cars).
Maximum Speed: 300 km/h.
Built: 1992-1993 by GEC-Alsthom/Brush/ANF/De Dietrich/BN Construction/ACEC.
Note: DM vehicles carry the set numbers indicated below.

10-Car Sets. Built for services starting from/terminating at London Waterloo. Individual vehicles in each set are allocated numbers 373xxx0 + 373xxx1 + 373xxx2 + 373xxx3 + 373xxx4 + 373xxx5 + 373xxx6 + 373xxx8 + 373xxx9, where 3xxx denotes the set number.

Non-standard Livery: 0 – grey with silver ends, TGV symbol and green or blue doors.

373xxx0 series. DM. Lot No. 31118 1992–1995. 68.5 t.
373xxx1 series. MS. Lot No. 31119 1992–1995. –/48 2T. 44.6 t.
373xxx2 series. TS. Lot No. 31120 1992–1995. –/58 1T. 28.1 t.
373xxx3 series. TS. Lot No. 31121 1992–1995. –/58 1T. 29.7 t.
373xxx4 series. TS. Lot No. 31122 1992–1995. –/58 1T. 28.3 t.
373xxx5 series. TS. Lot No. 31123 1992–1995. –/58 2T. 29.2 t.
373xxx6 series. RB. Lot No.31124 1992–1995. 31.1 t.
373xxx7 series. TF. Lot No. 31125 1992–1995. 39/– 1T. 29.6 t.
373xxx8 series.TF. Lot No. 31126 1992–1995. 39/– 1T. 32.2 t.
373xxx9 series.TBF. Lot No. 31127 1992–1995. 25/– 1TD. 39.4 t.

3001	**EU**	EU	*EU*	NP	3006	**EU**	EU	*EU*	NP
3002	**EU**	EU	*EU*	NP	3007	**EU**	EU	*EU*	NP
3003	**EU**	EU	*EU*	NP	3008	**EU**	EU	*EU*	NP
3004	**EU**	EU	*EU*	NP	3009	**EU**	EU	*EU*	NP
3005	**EU**	EU	*EU*	NP	3010	**EU**	EU	*EU*	NP

3011	**EU**	EU	*EU*	NP	3207*	**EU**	SF	*EU*	LY
3012	**EU**	EU	*EU*	NP	3208*	**EU**	SF	*EU*	LY
3013	**EU**	EU	*EU*	NP	3209*	**EU**	SF	*EU*	LY
3014	**EU**	EU	*EU*	NP	3210*	**EU**	SF	*EU*	LY
3015	**EU**	EU	*EU*	NP	3211	**EU**	SF	*EU*	LY
3016	**EU**	EU	*EU*	NP	3212	**EU**	SF	*EU*	LY
3017	**EU**	EU	*EU*	NP	3213	**EU**	SF	*EU*	LY
3018	**EU**	EU	*EU*	NP	3214	**EU**	SF	*EU*	LY
3019	**EU**	EU	*EU*	NP	3215*	**EU**	SF	*EU*	LY
3020	**EU**	EU	*EU*	NP	3216*	**EU**	SF	*EU*	LY
3021	**EU**	EU	*EU*	NP	3217	**EU**	SF	*EU*	LY
3022	**EU**	EU	*EU*	NP	3218	**EU**	SF	*EU*	LY
3101	**EU**	SB	*EU*	FF	3219	**EU**	SF	*EU*	LY
3102	**EU**	SB	*EU*	FF	3220	**EU**	SF	*EU*	LY
3103	**EU**	SB	*EU*	FF	3221	**EU**	SF	*EU*	LY
3104	**EU**	SB	*EU*	FF	3222	**EU**	SF	*EU*	LY
3105	**EU**	SB	*EU*	FF	3223*	**EU**	SF	*EU*	LY
3106	**EU**	SB	*EU*	FF	3224*	**EU**	SF	*EU*	LY
3107	**EU**	SB	*EU*	FF	3225*	**0**	SF	*EU*	LY
3108	**EU**	SB	*EU*	FF	3226*	**0**	SF	*EU*	LY
3201 *	**EU**	SF	*EU*	LY	3227*	**0**	SF	*EU*	LY
3202 *	**EU**	SF	*EU*	LY	3228*	**0**	SF	*EU*	LY
3203 *	**0**	SF	*EU*	LY	3229*	**EU**	SF	*EU*	LY
3204 *	**0**	SF	*EU*	LY	3230*	**EU**	SF	*EU*	LY
3205	**EU**	SF	*EU*	LY	3231	**EU**	SF	*EU*	LY
3206	**EU**	SF	*EU*	LY	3232	**EU**	SF	*EU*	LY

8-Car Sets. Built for Regional Eurostar services. Individual vehicles in each set are allocated numbers 373xxx0 + 373xxx1 + 373xxx3 + 373xxx2 + 373xxx5 + 373xxx6 + 373xxx7 + 373xxx9, where 3xxx denotes the set number.

3733xx0 series. DM. 68.5 t.
3733xx1 series. MS. –/48 1T. 44.6 t.
3733xx3 series. TS. –/58 2T. 29.7 t.
3733xx2 series. TS. –/58 1T. 28.1 t.
3733xx5 series. TS. –/58 1T. 29.2 t.
3733xx6 series. RB. 31.1 t.
3733xx7 series. TF. 39/– 1T. 29.6 t.
3733xx9 series. TBF. 18/– 1TD. 39.4 t.

3301	**GN**	EU	*GN*	NP	3308	**EU**	EU		NP
3302	**GN**	EU	*GN*	NP	3309	**EU**	EU	*GN*	NP
3303	**GN**	EU	*GN*	NP The White Rose	3310	**EU**	EU	*GN*	NP
3304	**GN**	EU	*GN*	NP The White Rose	3311	**EU**	EU	*GN*	NP
3305	**GN**	EU	*GN*	NP Yorkshire Forward	3312	**EU**	EU	*GN*	NP
3306	**GN**	EU	*GN*	NP Golden Jubilee	3313	**EU**	EU	*GN*	NP
3307	**EU**	EU		NP	3314	**EU**	EU	*GN*	NP

Spare DM:

3999	**EU**	EU		NP

4. SERVICE UNITS

CLASS 930/0   SANDITE/DE-ICING UNIT

Converted from Class 405.

Formation: DMB–DMB.
Supply System: 750 V DC third rail.
Traction Motors: Two English Electric 507 of 185 kW.
Construction: Steel.   **Doors:** Slam.
Gangways: Within unit.   **Bogies:** Central 43 inch.
Couplers: Buckeye.   **Maximum Speed:** 75 m.p.h.
Braking: Tread brakes.   **Dimensions:** 19.05 x 2.74 m.
Multiple Working: SR type.

975586/975587/975605. DMB. Lot No. 3231 Southern Railway Eastleigh 1947. 39.0 t.
975588/975589/975595/975598/975600/975602/975603. DMB. Lot No. 1060. Southern Railway Eastleigh 1941. 39.0 t.
975590/975591/975601. DMB. Lot No. 3384 Eastleigh 1948. 39.0 t.
975594. DMB. Lot No. 3618 Eastleigh 1950. 39.0 t.
975896/975897. DMB. Lot No. 3506 Eastleigh 1950. 39.0 t.

930 002	**RK**	NR	SE	RM	975896	(11387)	975897	(11388)
930 003	**RO**	NR	SE	RM	975594	(12658)	975595	(10994)
930 004	**RO**	NR	SE	RM	975586	(10907)	975587	(10908)
930 006	**RO**	NR	SE	RM	975590	(10833)	975591	(10834)
930 010	**RK**	MA		DY	975600	(10988)	975601	(10843)
930 011	**RK**	NR	SE	RM	975602	(10991)	975603	(10992)
Spare	RO	NR		AF	975598	(10989)	975605	(10940)

CLASS 930/0   ROUTE LEARNING UNIT

Converted from Class 411/4 (No. 1505).

Formation: DM–TB–DM.
Supply System: 750 V DC third rail.
Traction Motors: Two English Electric 507 of 185 kW.
Construction: Steel.   **Doors:** Slam.
Gangways: Within unit.   **Bogies:** Mk. 4/Commonwealth.
Couplers: Buckeye.   **Maximum Speed:** 90 m.p.h.
Braking: Tread brakes.   **Dimensions:** 20.34 x 2.82 m.
Multiple Working: SR type.

977861. DM. Lot No. 30111 Eastleigh 1956. 44.2 t.
977862. TB. Lot No. 30110 Eastleigh 1956. 36.2 t.
977863. DM. Lot No. 30108 Eastleigh 1956. 43.5 t.

930 082	**CX**	P	*SC*	SU	977861	(61044)	977862	(70039)
					977863	(61038)		

CLASS 930/1   TRACTOR UNIT

Converted from Class 416/2.

Formation: DMB–DMB.
Supply System: 750 V DC third rail.
Traction Motors: Two English Electric 507 of 185 kW.
Construction: Steel.   **Doors:** Slam.
Gangways: Within unit.   **Bogies:** Mk. 4 and Mk. 3B/Commonwealth.
Couplers: Buckeye.   **Maximum Speed:** 90 m.p.h.
Braking: Tread brakes.   **Dimensions:** 20.42 x 2.82 m.
Multiple Working: SR type.

977207. DMB. Lot No. 30388 Eastleigh 1958. 40.5 t.
977609. DMB. Lot No. 30617 Eastleigh 1961. 40.5 t.

930 101	N	NR		AF	977207	(61658)	977609	(65414)

CLASS 930/2   SANDITE/DE-ICING UNIT

Converted from Class 416/2.

Formation: DMB–DMB.
Supply System: 750 V DC third rail.
Traction Motors: Two English Electric 507 of 185 kW.
Construction: Steel.   **Doors:** Slam.
Gangways: Within unit.   **Bogies:** Mk. 3B.
Couplers: Buckeye.   **Maximum Speed:** 75 m.p.h.
Braking: Tread brakes.   **Dimensions:** 20.44 x 2.82 m.
Multiple Working: SR type.

977566/977567. DMB. Lot No. 30116 Eastleigh 1954–1955. 40.5 t.
977804/977864. DMB. Lot No. 30119 Eastleigh 1954. 40.5 t.
977805/977865/977871. DMB. Lot No. 30167 Eastleigh 1955. 40.5 t.
977872/977924/977925. DMB. Lot No. 30314. Eastleigh 1956–1958. 40.5 t.
977874/977875. DMB. Lot No. 30114 Eastleigh 1954. 40.5 t.

930 201	RK	NR	SE	RM	977566	(65312)	977567	(65314)
930 203	RK	NR	SE	RM	977864	(65341)	977865	(65355)
930 204	RK	NR	SE	RM	977874	(65302)	977875	(65304)
930 205	RO	NR	SE	RM	977871	(65353)	977872	(65367)
930 206	RK	NR	SE	RM	977924	(65382)	977925	(65379)

CLASS 931   TRACTOR UNIT

DM. Non gangwayed. Previously Class 419.

Formation: DM.
Supply System: 750 V DC third rail or battery power.
Traction Motors: Two English Electric 507 of 185 kW.
Construction: Steel.   **Doors:** Slam.

Gangways: Throughout.
Couplers: Buckeye.
Braking: Tread brakes.
Multiple Working: SR type.

Bogies: Mk. 3B.
Maximum Speed: 90 m.p.h.
Dimensions: 19.64 x 2.82 m.

68002. DM. Lot No. 30458 Eastleigh 1959. 45.5 t.

931 092   **N**   P   *SW*   BM   68002

CLASS 960/1   CAB SIGNALLING TEST UNITS

Converted from Class 309/2 units by Alstom Eastleigh 2001.

Supply System: 25 kV AC 50 Hz overhead.
BDTC–MBS–DTS. Gangwayed throughout.
Construction: Steel.
Traction Motors: Four GEC WT401 of 210 kW each.
Dimensions: 20.18 x 2.82 x 3.90 m.
Maximum Speed: 100 m.p.h.   **Doors**: Slam.
Couplings: Buckeye.   **Bogies**: Commonwealth.
Multiple Working: Within class.

Non-standard Livery: Light blue & white.

977962. BDTC. Lot No. 30679 York 1962. 40.0 t.
977965. BDTC. Lot No. 30675 York 1962. 40.0 t.
977963. MBS. Lot No. 30680 York 1962. 57.7 t.
977966. MBS. Lot No. 30676 York 1962. 57.7 t.
977964. DTS. Lot No. 30682 York 1962. 36.6 t.
977967. DTS. Lot No. 30678 York 1962. 36.6 t.

960 101	**0**	AM	*AM*	Old	977962	(75642)	977963	(61937)
				Dalby	977964	(75981)		
960 102	**0**	AM	*AM*	Old	977965	(75965)	977966	(61928)
				Dalby	977967	(75972)		

Names:

960 101 West Coast Flyer
960 102 New Dalby

CLASS 960/2   HITACHI TEST TRAIN

Converted from vehicles from Class 310 units 310 109 and 310 113 and Class 423 MBSO 62138. As we closed for press the vehicles were not yet formed as a complete unit or registered with Network Rail.
Further details awaited.

Non-standard Livery: All-over deep green.

960 201	**0**	HI		ZA	977977	(76137)	977978	(62090)
					977979	(62078)	977980	(76187)
					977981	(62138)		

5. EMUS AWAITING DISPOSAL

The list below comprises vehicles awaiting disposal which are stored on Network Rail, together with those stored at other locations which, although awaiting disposal, remain Network Rail registered.

Generally, units that are stored but where others in that class are still in service are listed in the main part of this book. This list mainly comprises classes of units of which there are none of that particular class still in revenue earning service.

25 kV AC 50 Hz Overhead Units:

309 613	**RN**	A	PY	75639	61934	71756	75978
309 617	**RN**	A	ZG	75643	61938		75982
309 623	**RN**	A	PY	75641	61927	71758	75980
309 627	**RN**	A	PY	75644	61931	70259	75975
310 046	**N**	H	PY	76130	62071	70731	76180
310 047	**N**	H	PY	76131	62072	70732	76181
310 049	**N**	H	KT	76133	62074	70734	76183
310 050	**N**	H	KT	76134	62075	70735	76184
310 051	**N**	H	KT	76135	62076	70736	76185
310 052	**N**	H	PY	76136	62077	70737	76186
310 057	**N**	H	PY	76141	62082	70742	76191
310 058	**N**	H	PY	76142	62083	70743	76192
310 059	**N**	H	KT	76143	62084	70744	76205
310 060	**N**	H	PY	76144	62085	70745	76194
310 064	**N**	H	PY	76148	62089	70749	76198
310 066	**N**	H	PY	76228	62091	70751	76200
310 067	**N**	H	PY	76151	62092	70752	76201
310 068	**N**	H	PY	76152	62093	70753	76202
310 069	**N**	H	PY	76153	62094	70754	76203
310 070	**N**	H	PY	76154	62095	70755	76204
310 074	**N**	H	PY	76145	62099	70759	76208
310 075	**N**	H	PY	76159	62100	70760	76209
310 084	**N**	H	PY	76168	62109	70769	76206
310 085	**N**	H	PY	76169	62110	70770	76219
310 088	**N**	H	PY	76172	62113	70773	76213
310 091	**N**	H	PY	76175	62116	70776	76225
310 095	**N**	H	PY	76179	62120	70779	
310 101	**RR**	H	PY	76157	62098		76207
310 102	**RR**	H	PY	76139	62080		76189
310 107	**RR**	H	PY	76146	62087		76196
310 108	**RR**	H	PY	76132	62073		76182
310 110	**RR**	H	PY	76138	62079		76188
310 111	**RR**	H	PY	76147	62088		76197
310 112	**RR**	H	PY	76140	62086		
310 113	**RR**	H	ZA	76158			76195

Spare Cars:

Cl. 303	**S**	A	PY	61816	75624	75773	75824	
Cl. 307	**BG**	MD	KT	75023				
Cl. 308	**N**	A	PY	70612	70621	70622	70631	70640
	WY	A	PY	75881				
Cl. 309	**RN**	A	PY	70256	71760			
	RN	A	ZG	71759				
Cl. 310	**RR**	H	PY	76156	76190	76193	76218	

750 V DC Third Rail Units:

417	**B**	CM	KT	76301	70826	70860	76302
4308	**N**	H	PY	61275	75395		
5001	**G**	H	KT	14001	15101	15207	14002
6213	**BG**	NR	PY	65327	77512		
6308	**N**	NR	PY	14564	16108		
6309	**N**	NR	PY	14562	16106		
932 620	**0**	AM	ZG	61948	70653	70660	61949

Spare Cars:

Cl. 411	**ST**	AM	ZG	69343	
Cl. 416	**I**	NR	ZG	977296	(65319)
Cl. 424	**0**	BT	ZD	76112	
Cl. 438	**B**	CM	KT	70812	
	N	X	ZG	977764	(70866)

6. CODES

6.1. LIVERY CODES

Code Description

AL	Advertising livery (see class heading for details).
B	BR blue.
BG	BR blue & grey lined out in white.
C2	c2c Rail (blue with metallic grey doors & pink c2c branding).
CB	Old Connex South Eastern (NSE blue with a yellow lower bodyside).
CO	Centro (grey/green with light blue, white & yellow stripes).
CN	New Connex South Eastern (white with yellow doors, black window surrounds & grey lower band).
CX	Connex (white with yellow lower body & blue solebar).
EU	Eurostar (white with dark blue & yellow stripes).
FS	First Group corporate regional/suburban livery (indigo blue with pink & white stripes).
G	BR Southern Region/SR or BR green.
GA	South Central "Heritage" EMUs (white & dark green with light green semi-circular patches at cab ends. Light green stripe along length of unit).
GE	First Great Eastern (grey, green, blue & white).
GM	Greater Manchester PTE (light grey/dark grey with red & white stripes).
GN	Great North Eastern Railway (dark blue with a red stripe).
GV	Gatwick Express EMU (red, white & indigo blue with mauve & blue doors).
GX	Gatwick Express IC (dark grey/white/burgundy/white).
HE	Heathrow Express (silver grey & indigo blue with black window surrounds).
I	BR InterCity (dark grey/white/red/white).
IL	Island Line (light blue, with illustrations featuring dinosaurs etc).
ME	Refurbished Merseyrail Electrics (metallic silver with yellow doors).
MT	Old Merseytravel (yellow/white with grey & black stripes).
MY	New Merseytravel (yellow/white with yellow stripe).
N	BR Network South East (white & blue with red lower bodyside stripe, grey solebar & cab ends).
NT	BR Network South East (white & blue with red lower bodyside & cantrail stripes).
NW	North Western Trains/First North Western (blue with gold cant rail stripe & star).
O	Non-standard livery (see class heading for details).
RK	Railtrack (green & blue).
RM	Royal Mail (red with yellow stripes above solebar).
RN	North West Regional Railways (dark blue/grey with green & white stripes).
RO	Old Railtrack (orange with white & grey stripes).
RR	Regional Railways (dark blue/grey with light blue & white stripes, three narrow dark blue stripes at cab ends).
S	Old Strathclyde PTE (orange & black lined out in white).
SC	New Strathclyde PTE (carmine & cream lined out in black & gold).

SD	South West Trains outer suburban livery (deep blue with red doors & orange & red cab sides).
SL	Silverlink (indigo blue with white stripe, green lower body & yellow doors).
SN	South Central (white & dark green with light green patch near cab ends).
SP	New Strathclyde PTE Class 170/334 livery (carmine & cream, with a turquoise stripe).
ST	Stagecoach (white & blue with orange & red stripes).
SW	South West Trains (long-distance stock) (white & dark blue with black window surrounds, red doors & red panel with orange stripe at unit ends).
SX	Stansted Express (two-tone metallic blue with grey doors).
TR	Thameslink Rail (dark blue with a broad orange stripe & two narrower white bodyside stripes plus white cantrail stripe).
U	Plain white or grey undercoat.
VT	New Virgin Trains (silver, with black window surrounds, white cantrail stripe & red roof. Red is swept down at unit ends).
WN	Old West Anglia Great Northern (white with blue, grey & orange stripes).
WP	New West Anglia Great Northern (deep purple with white doors).
WY	Old West Yorkshire PTE (red/cream with thin yellow stripe).
YN	West Yorkshire PTE (red with light grey N).

6.2. OWNER CODES

Operation   Description

A	Angel Trains
AM	Alstom
BT	Bombardier Transportation
CD	Cotswold Rail
CM	Cambrian Trains
E	English Welsh & Scottish Railway
EU	Eurostar (UK)
GB	GB Rail
H	HSBC Rail (UK)
HI	Hitachi
HE	British Airports Authority
NR	Network Rail
MA	Maintrain
MD	Ministry of Defence
P	Porterbrook Leasing Company
RM	Royal Mail
SB	SNCB/NMBS (Société Nationale des Chemins de fer Belges/ Nationale Maatschappij der belgische Spoorwegen)
SF	SNCF (Société Nationale des Chemins de fer Français)
X	Sold for scrap/further use and awaiting collection or owner unknown.

6.3. OPERATOR CODES

Code	Operator
Code	*Operator*
AM	Alstom
AN	Arriva Trains Northern
C2	c2c Rail
CT	Central Trains
E	English Welsh & Scottish Railway
EU	Eurostar (UK)
GE	First Great Eastern.
GN	Great North Eastern Raiway
GX	Gatwick Express
HE	Heathrow Express
IL	Island Line
ME	Merseyrail Electrics (Serco/Netherlands Railways)
NW	First North Western
SC	South Central
SE	South Eastern Trains
SL	Silverlink
SO	Serco Railtest
SR	ScotRail
SS	Normally used only on special or charter services
SW	South West Trains
TR	Thameslink Rail
VW	Virgin West Coast
WN	West Anglia Great Northern

6.4. ALLOCATION & LOCATION CODES

Code	Location	Operator
AF	Ashford Chart Leacon (Kent)	Bombardier Transportation
BD	Birkenhead North	Merseyrail Electrics
BI	Brighton	South Central
BM	Bournemouth	South West Trains
BY	Bletchley	Silverlink
CC	Clacton	*Storage location only*
CE	Crewe International Electric	EWS
CT*	MoD Caerwent AFD (Chepstow)	Ministry of Defence
DY	Derby Etches Park	Maintrain
EM	East Ham	c2c
FF	Forest (Brussels)	SNCB/NMBS
FR	Fratton	South West Trains
GI	Gillingham (Kent)	South Eastern Trains
GW	Shields Road (Glasgow)	ScotRail
HE	Hornsey (London)	West Anglia Great Northern
IL	Ilford (London)	First Great Eastern

KT	MoD Kineton (Warwickshire)	Ministry of Defence
LG	Longsight Electric (Manchester)	First North Western
LY	Le Landy (Paris)	SNCF
MA	Manchester Longsight	West Coast Traincare
MM	Fire Service College, Moreton-in-Marsh	Cotswold Rail
NC	Norwich Crown Point	Anglia Railways
NL	Neville Hill T&RSMD (Leeds)	Arriva Trains Northern/Maintrain
NP	North Pole International (London)	Eurostar (UK)
NT	Northam (Southampton)	Siemens/South West Trains
OH	Old Oak Common EMUs (London)	Heathrow Express
PY	MoD DERA Shoeburyness	Ministry of Defence
RM	Ramsgate	South Eastern Trains
RY	Ryde (Isle of Wight)	Island Line
SG	Slade Green (London)	South Eastern Trains
SI	Soho (Birmingham)	Maintrain
SL	Stewarts Lane (London)	Gatwick Express/VSOE
SU	Selhurst (Croydon)	South Central
WD	Wimbledon	South West Trains
ZA	RTC Business Park (Derby)	Serco Railtest/AEA Technology
ZB	Doncaster Works	Wabtec
ZC	Crewe Works	Bombardier Transportation
ZD	Derby Litchurch Lane Works	Bombardier Transportation
ZF	Doncaster Works	Bombardier Transportation
ZG	Eastleigh Works	Alstom
ZH	Springburn Works Glasgow	Alstom
ZI	Ilford Works	Bombardier Transportation
ZK	Kilmarnock Works	Hunslet Barclay
ZN	Wolverton Works	Alstom
ZP	Horbury (Wakefield)	Bombardier Transportation

* = unofficial code.

ABBREVIATIONS

AFD	Air Force Department
DERA	Defence Evaluation & Research Agency